NINTH EDITION

100th Congress
Approved
98th Congress,
1st Session,
S. Con. Res. 35,
Passed July 27, 1983
S. Doc. 99–17

THE CAPITOL

A PICTORIAL HISTORY OF THE CAPITOL AND OF THE CONGRESS

WASHINGTON, *in the Territory of* COLUMBIA.

A PREMIUM

OF a LOT in this City, to be deſignated by impartial judges, and FIVE HUNDRED DOLLARS; or a MEDAL of that value, at the option of the party; will be given by the Commiſſioners of the Federal Buildings, to the perſon who, before the fifteenth day of July, 1792, ſhall produce to them the moſt approved PLAN, if adopted by them, for a CAPITOL, to be erected in this City; and TWO HUNDRED AND FIFTY DOLLARS, or a MEDAL, for the Plan deemed next in merit to the one they ſhall adopt.   The building to be of brick, and to contain the following apartments, to wit:

A Conference Room
A Room for the Repreſentatives } ſufficient to accommodate 300 perſons each. theſe rooms to be of full elevation.
A Lobby or Antichamber to the latter
A Senate Room of 1200 ſquare feet area
An Antichamber or Lobby to the laſt

12 Rooms of 600 ſquare feet area each, for Committee Rooms and Clerks' Offices, to be of half the elevation of the former.

Drawings will be expected of the ground plats, elevations of each front, and ſections through the building in ſuch directions as may be neceſſary to explain the internal ſtructure; and an eſtimate of the cubic feet of brick-work compoſing the whole maſs of the walls.

March 14, 1792   *tf.*   THE COMMISSIONERS.

Contents

Foreword

The Joint Committee on Printing is pleased to present this ninth edition of *The Capitol,* which contains history of the Capitol and the Congress of the United States. Publication of this book was initiated during the 84th Congress by the late Sam Rayburn of Texas, Speaker of the House of Representatives. Then, as now, it focuses on both the Capitol as a historic edifice and the Congress as a living and dynamic institution within our Federal Government.

The Capitol, with its massive cast iron dome, commands worldwide attention as the symbol of our democracy. Its construction was begun in 1793, when President George Washington laid the cornerstone on Jenkins Hill, a spot that was described by Major Pierre Charles L'Enfant as a "pedestal waiting for a monument". It was first occupied in 1800, when the national government moved to Washington from Philadelphia. Since those early days, the Capitol has been destroyed, rebuilt, restored, extended, domed and re-domed.

The Capitol is the place where Members of Congress meet to form the laws of our Nation, where our Presidents are inaugurated and where the President's annual State of the Union message is given. The great rotunda is revered as the place where deceased national leaders and fallen heroes lie in state.

However, in addition to housing our national legislature and other official functions, the Capitol is also a museum filled with artistic and historic treasures. Great national events and past political leaders are depicted in the many paintings and pieces of statuary throughout the Capitol. These are inspiring reminders of our forebears and their contributions to the growth of this great Nation. Millions of tourists from every State in the Union and around the world visit the Capitol each year. The Capitol belongs to each and every one of them as the home and emblem of a free nation.

On behalf of the Members of the Joint Committee on Printing, we hope that you will find this publication to be both an enjoyable and an informative depiction of this important national symbol.

Representative Frank Annunzio
Chairman
Joint Committee on Printing

Senator Wendell H. Ford
Vice Chairman
Joint Committee on Printing

The Capitol—Its History and Architecture

Symbol of The Power of The People

The Capitol of the United States represents Government of the people, by the people, and for the people.

Inception and Construction

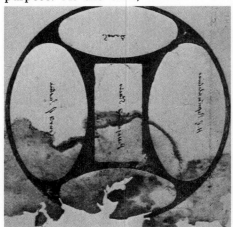

The announcement for
the Capitol competition
of 1792 offered a lot in
the city and $500 for
the winning design.

Thomas Jefferson
oversaw both
competitions for the
construction of the
Capitol and the White
House. This sketch
was probably done
about 1799 by
Benjamin Latrobe, the
second Architect of the
Capitol.

The genesis of the Capitol is found in the Constitution of the United States adopted by our forebears in 1787. Article I, Section 8, Clause 17 provides that the Federal Government settle in a permanent home in a district "not exceeding 10 miles square." Congress passed legislation in 1790 to establish a permanent residence for the Federal Government, and authorized President George Washington to appoint three commissioners to oversee the design of the city and the construction of necessary government buildings by the year 1800. Much controversy developed between northern and southern interests over a suitable location for the capital city before the site on the Potomac near Georgetown was finally agreed to. A talented French engineer, Pierre Charles L'Enfant, was employed to develop the plan for the new City of Washington including the location of the Federal buildings. L'Enfant was also to design the Capitol and the White House and to oversee their construction. For the Capitol, L'Enfant selected an elevated position overlooking the public grounds of the Mall and devised a plan for the City's major avenues to converge on the site, thus giving it unrivaled prominence and visibility.

L'Enfant's temperament, unfortunately, placed him in frequent conflict with his associates and superiors on the actual plan for the Capitol. One of these associates was Squire Daniel Carroll, an original landowner in the Federal District, who decided to build a new manor house in the path of one of the great avenues that L'Enfant envisioned to radiate in all directions from the Capitol. Unwilling to accept this intrusion on his grand design, L'Enfant sent a work crew to demolish the unfinished building which stood in the way of what would become New Jersey Avenue Southeast. But Squire Carroll's uncle was one of the three Commissioners charged with the development of the City. This conflict, combined with other disputes between L'Enfant and the Commissioners, led to his dismissal in 1792.

In the fall of 1792, the Commissioners of the District of Columbia announced a competition which would award $500 and a city lot to the architect with the best design for the Capitol. While this competition produced some interesting ideas, the 16 known entries were unable to produce a plan that seemed appropriate to the building's complex function and symbolic purpose. At the time, America's few

Although Thomas
Jefferson did not enter
the competition for the
Capitol he did draw this
idealized plan. A
student of antiquity, he
used the Pantheon in
Rome, as the basis for
his study.

architects were mostly self-trained men whose experience was limited primarily to homes and small-scale public buildings. Neither President Washington nor Secretary of State Thomas Jefferson was satisfied with the results at the competition's deadline.

In November of the same year, William Thornton, a young multi-talented physician, wrote to the Commissioners of the Federal District, asking permission to submit a late entry. Thornton's request was granted and he submitted his design to President Washington in 1793. Thornton's sketch reflected the style and spirit of the Palladian architecture of early 18th century England. He succeeded in producing a dignified, yet small-scale, design that was thought to be within the means of a young, but architecturally ambitious, nation. President Washington was immediately impressed with the design and recom-

mended the plan for its "grandeur, simplicity, and convenience." Thomas Jefferson eagerly concurred. The finished version of his design delighted everyone except the runner-up, Stephen Hallet, a French-born architect who had seemed assured of winning the competition before Thornton's entry was submitted. As compensation, Hallet was awarded $500 and placed in charge of the actual construction of the Capitol.

After resolving some structural details, President Washington formally approved Thornton's design and on September 18, 1793, he laid the Capitol's cornerstone in a Masonic ceremony in company with local officials. After the ceremony, in which the cornerstone was placed on an engraved silver plate, an ox was roasted on a spit and the assembled multitude ate and drank heartily until dusk. This event was both the first and last recorded occasion on which the corner-

Stephen Hallet was the runner-up for the Capitol competition (1792). This elevation shows the basic idea for the building's eventual construction. Thornton may have seen Hallet's work before making his own winning design.

This design for the east front was drawn by Dr. Thornton and approved by George Washington. The wing on the right was completed first.

stone, with its engraved silver plate, was seen. In 1958, during the extension of the east front, a determined, but unsuccessful, effort was made to locate the stone and plate.

Construction of the Capitol proceeded steadily after the festivities of the cornerstone-laying were over. Throughout this period a conflict was brewing between Dr. Thornton, who sought to preserve his design intact, and Stephen Hallet, the supervisor of construction, who began to introduce subtle changes in the design which were reminiscent of his own rejected plan. Thornton forced a confrontation, and the outraged Hallet was dismissed in 1794. The next superintendent of construction was George Hadfield, who arrived in 1795. Almost immediately he came under Dr. Thornton's criticism. Hadfield, though talented and dedicated, overstepped his authority, and he was dismissed 3 years later. James Hoban, who is best remembered as architect of the White House, succeeded Hadfield as superintendent. In 1800 Congress was installed in the one completed wing of the Capitol.

In 1803 President Jefferson appointed Benjamin Latrobe, an academically trained architect, to oversee the continuing construction of the Capitol. Since December of 1802 the House had been meeting in a temporary brick structure thrown up hastily on the foundations of its own wing. One story tall, oval, and unbearably hot three seasons of the year, this structure was called "the Oven" by the Representatives who were unfortunate enough to meet in it. One of Latrobe's first acts was to order the demolition of "the Oven," and to raise the walls of the House wing. Work on it proceeded smoothly under Latrobe's guidance, but his prolific production of designs for other public and private buildings frequently directed his attention away from Washington, engendering considerable criticism. In response, he appointed a fellow Englishman, John Lenthal, to be Clerk of the Works, with day-to-day responsibility for the Capitol when he was away. Lenthal took charge of the work with vigor, competence and ability, but during one of Latrobe's extended absences in 1808, he removed the supports for the vaulting in the Supreme Court Chamber prematurely. The massive arches collapsed, killing Lenthal.

Upon the completion of the House wing, Latrobe substantially rebuilt the Senate wing which was plagued with leaks and falling plaster, although less than 10 years old. His revised plan created the Supreme Court Chamber and a handsome two-story Senate Chamber directly above it.

Under Latrobe's continued supervision, the House and Senate wings of the Capitol were virtually finished by 1811. Yet, due to the imminence of war with Great Britain, the general appropriations for work on the Capitol ceased, and all plans for further improvement were put aside. In August of 1814 a British fleet appeared in the Chesapeake Bay with the determined purpose of capturing Washington. They brushed aside the opposing American militiamen at Bladensburg, Maryland and on the 24th of that month, marched into the Federal City. One of the British commanders, Rear Admiral Cockburn, led his men into the House Chamber, jumped up onto the Speaker's chair and called the troops around him. Mocking legislative procedure, he asked the soldiers: "Shall this harbor of Yankee democracy be burned? All

On September 18, 1793, President George Washington laid the Capitol's cornerstone. The event was captured by artist Allyn Cox in this painting located on the first floor corridor of the House wing (1974).

This is the Capitol when first occupied by Congress in 1800.

for it say 'aye'." The Admiral's question was affirmed unanimously, and the British troops set a great bonfire by piling desks, carpets, books, paintings and everything else movable in the center of the Chamber, ensuring a good blaze by sprinkling gunpowder over the pile before setting the torch to both wings. Late in the evening a violent thunderstorm drenched the burning buildings, saving them from total destruction.

Latrobe made several drawings that showed the extent of the damage, and then proceeded with reconstruction of the Capitol. Latrobe used that opportunity to alter Thornton's plan to his own tastes and to better accommodate a growing Congress. He set to work with characteristic vigor, designing an enlarged Senate Chamber and a handsome semicircular room for the House of Representatives, which today is Statuary Hall. During the reconstruction, Congress met in a building where the Supreme Court now stands. This structure, the "Brick Capitol," was hastily erected in 1815 at the expense of some of the city's businessmen who feared that Congress would move the seat of Government away from the District of Columbia.

After Latrobe's resignation in 1817, Charles Bulfinch of Boston became the third architect to shape the Capitol. Widely respected for his designs, which included the State Houses for Massachusetts and Connecticut and a number of hospitals, Bulfinch also appears to have possessed the tact and political sensitivity

his predecessors had lacked. He served as Architect from 1818 until the Capitol was completed in 1829, when the position of Architect of the Capitol was abolished. It was Bulfinch who completed the central section of the building, including the lower walls of the handsome rotunda familiar to tourists today. Although some of his work involved the construction of Latrobe's designs, the west central building and the original rotunda and dome are exclusively Bulfinch's handiwork. Much criticism had been directed at the low height of the rotunda dome as originally planned, and Bulfinch prepared several drawings of alternate solutions to the problem, including one dome of considerably greater height merely as a point of comparison. Upon submission of these designs to the

The burning of the Capitol depicted in a mural by Allyn Cox, in the House corridor (1974).

This original drawing of the Capitol depicts the damage it sustained when it was burned by the British during the War of 1812.

Benjamin Latrobe proposed a Propylea type entrance for the west front. Subsequently this part of the Capitol was redesigned by Bulfinch.

For nearly 50 years this is where the Representatives met. This painting by Samuel F.B. Morse shows a night session of the House in 1822. The thick draperies deadened unwanted echoes.

This is the earliest known photograph of the Capitol. It is a daguerreotype and was probably taken by John Plumbe, Jr., reproduced in a lithographic print (called a Plumbeotype) and published around 1846. Water for nonculinary purposes was stored in the cistern seen in the center foreground.

Cabinet, the taller dome was selected because it was more prominent, despite Bulfinch's personal distaste for the height. He was ordered to go ahead with construction of the higher dome, built of masonry and wood with copper sheathing.

During the reconstruction after the fire of 1814, Congress decided to assign watchmen to keep strangers from wandering throughout the Capitol and grounds at night. Three watchmen and one sergeant were hired in 1825. They constituted the first police force in the Federal District outside Georgetown, and were the forerunners of today's U.S. Capitol Police. These early watchmen served also as guides in the Capitol. With the influx of visitors from the Centennial Exposition in Philadelphia in 1876, a separate guide force was recruited, thus beginning the present day guide service.

In 1824 the Marquis de Lafayette, hero of the Revolution, returned to America for his first visit in 40 years. The great general was given a warm welcome everywhere he traveled in the country, but nowhere was it more spontaneous or heartfelt than in the Chamber of the House of Representatives, where he was received by the Members on December 9, 1824. Unprompted, they rose to their feet to honor him, and then, as though 200 men were a single person, they doffed their hats. This was a remarkable tribute according to the customs of the day. Members of Congress usually re-moved their hats only in the presence of the President, a reigning monarch, clergyman or, of course, when meeting a lady. The rules of the House no longer allow hats to be worn in the Chamber.

Benjamin Latrobe's design for the reconstructed Capitol had included an important innovation, the Capitol's first sanitary facilities. Originally the Congress was accommodated for nearly two decades with facilities outside the building. In the delicate language of the time, they were known as "necessaries." Latrobe, with characteristic ingenuity, provided water closets in the courtyards and in the Capitol. Water was carried to the roof of the building from nearby cisterns and poured down the drains, which emptied at the foot of Capitol Hill. Before the city had a water system a large circular cistern on the east front was kept filled with water for nonculinary use.

Washington was a small town, with little in the way of entertainment other than the business of legislation and Government. Consequently, viewing the Congress while in session was one of the most important and liveliest diversions of the day. Ladies frequently spent their afternoons in the House and Senate visitors' galleries watching the parliamentary maneuvering and debates. The Senate, in particular, was considered worthy of attendance. Henry Clay, John C. Calhoun and Daniel Webster, three of the greatest orators in our history, were all

Members of the Senate in the decades before 1850. On the day a burning issue was to be debated, the galleries in the Senate would begin to fill in the morning. When the time came for the debate to begin, the more gallant Members of the Senate would give up their desks to the belles who could not crowd their way into the galleries. On warm days the poorly ventilated Chamber would heat up quickly, and fruit and beverages were sometimes passed on long poles to the sweltering spectators.

Sam Houston, the father of Texas' independence and statehood, was a colorful Senator of this era. He would lounge at his desk with the casual air of a frontiersman, whittling delicate wooden hearts which he passed up to the loveliest ladies in the gallery. He disdained the black broadcloth tail coats favored by many of his colleagues in favor of a more flamboyant wardrobe. A visitor once noted that his costume included a panther-skin vest, a brightly striped serape slung over his shoulder and a generous sombrero.

The House of Representatives had its own colorful personalities in those lively years. One of the best-remembered was John Randolph of Virginia, a member of the famous family that provided both the Old Dominion and the United States with a number of outstanding public servants. John Randolph served in either the House or the Senate almost continuously from 1799 until his death in 1833, but his first love was always hunting. At the height of the hunting season, it was his regular practice to ride to the hounds from dawn until the hour the House session began. At the appointed time, he would gallop to the Capitol leaving his lathered horse with grooms. Randolph would then stride into the House Chamber, still clothed in mud-spattered boots and red hunting coat, with a pack of hounds padding along at his heels.

During those years the atmosphere within the grand space of the rotunda was also far different from its present august dignity. Numerous vendors hawked items ranging from

The crypt with its 40 Doric columns supports the rotunda which is directly above it. It was built by Bulfinch with walls and columns of sandstone.

An oil painting by an unknown artist depicts the Capitol from Pennsylvania Avenue about 1827.

An 1842 session in the Senate is illustrated in this old print, one of many references consulted for the restoration of the Chamber in 1976.

Clio, the Muse of History, in her chariot, notes significant events as they transpire. The clock was once the official timepiece of the House.

food to souvenirs. Petitioners and officeseekers trailed Congressmen as they moved in and out of the legislative Chambers and committee rooms. Temporary exhibits displaying the latest innovations in science, agriculture or industry attracted various passers-by. In both House and Senate restaurants, refreshments were liberally and regularly enjoyed by thirsty legislators, despite the fact that the American Congressional Temperance Society had been established in the House Chamber in 1833. A few years later, the Senate voted to ban the sale of hard liquor in the Capitol. The House refused to go along, and for seven years the Senate abided by its own resolution while the other side of the building continued to flow with strong drink.

The most pervasive habit of the time, if we are to accept accounts of contemporary European travelers in America, was the use of tobacco in the form of chewing or snuff. Both men and women seem to have enjoyed those forms of tobacco. Charles Dickens wrote: "Washington may be called the headquarters of tobacco tinctured saliva. . . . In all public places of America, this filthy custom is recognized."

One thing foreign visitors did agree upon was the grandeur of the Capitol itself. Mrs. Frances Trollope, an English writer noted for her acid pen, appeared to be happily surprised by the building:

"Our first object the next morning was to get sight of the Capitol, and our impatience sent us forth before breakfast. The mists of morning still hung around this magnificent building when first it broke upon our view, and I am not sure that the effect produced was not the greater for this circumstance. At all events, we were struck with admiration and surprise. None of us, I believe, expected to see so imposing a structure on that side of the Atlantic. I am ill at describing buildings, but the beauty and majesty of the American capitol might defy an abler pen than mine to do it justice. It stands so finely, too, high and alone.

"The magnificent western facade is approached from the city by terraces and steps of bolder proportions than I ever before saw. The elegant eastern front, to which many persons give the preference, is on a level with a newly-planted, but exceedingly handsome enclosure, which in a few years, will offer the shade of all the most splendid trees which flourish in the Union. . . ."

The Capitol was the scene of many "firsts" in American history. In 1829, in a ceremony open to the public, Andrew Jackson became the first President to be inaugurated on the east front steps. Until that time chief executives had been installed either in the Senate or House of Representatives' Chamber, with only invited guests being admitted. Old Hickory would have none of that. He had been elected as a man of the people and he was determined to have his installation open to everyone. Most recently, the inauguration of President Reagan in 1981 was the first for the west front of the Capitol, and in 1985, the sub-zero weather drove the inauguration indoors to the rotunda for the first time. On January 30, 1835, President Jackson was the first victim of an assassination attempt at the Capitol. As he was leaving funeral services in the Capitol to return to the White House, a man accosted him, raised a pistol, and fired point blank at the President. The weapon misfired. Jackson, no stranger to a good scuffle, went after the would-be assassin with his cane. A second pistol also misfired, and the President and a Navy lieutenant succeeded in disarming the assailant.

John Quincy Adams has the distinction of being one of two Presidents who was elected to Congress after leaving the White House. The

In 1829 Andrew Jackson was inaugurated as the seventh President of the United States on the east front steps of the Capitol. This event was captured in a painting by artist Allyn Cox in the first floor corridor of the House wing (1974).

14

other, Andrew Johnson, was elected to the Senate but served only a short time before his death. Adams continued to serve with great distinction for 17 years. He was stricken on the floor of the House in 1848 while delivering an impassioned attack on the treaty which had just ended the Mexican War. The old patriot was carried from the floor to a sofa in the Speaker's office where he died 2 days later. The Capitol was shrouded in mourning from its base to the summit of the elevated lantern in the dome. A bronze disc was set into the floor of the old House Chamber to mark the site of his desk. It remains today, not only as a tribute to Adams, but also to mark the famous "whispering spot" where words spoken softly can be heard all the way across the room.

The Capitol is seldom thought of as a scientific laboratory, but it was there in 1844 that Samuel F.B. Morse first demonstrated the telegraph. Forty miles of wire had been strung to Baltimore, where his assistant waited with a receiving set. Morse tapped out the historic message: "What hath God wrought?" From Baltimore, Morse's assistant stoically flashed in return, "What is the news in Washington?"

By 1850 it was apparent that Congress was outgrowing the Capitol. When Dr. Thornton had submitted his design in 1793, the Senate consisted of 30 Members, and the House 106. The results of the 1850 census caused the House to be enlarged to 237 Members, and the 31 States of the Union sent 62 Senators to Washington. Thus, Congress had more than doubled, and the country had spread across the continent. It was obvious that the Capitol would have to be enlarged. Senator Jefferson Davis of Mississippi, who

became President of the Confederacy, served as a persuasive spokesman for those Members of both Houses favoring expansion. In September of 1850 Congress appropriated funds for design and construction of two large new wings. The architect chosen for the new wings was Thomas U. Walter of Philadelphia, who later supervised construction of an addition to the Treasury Building near the White House. Massachusetts and Maryland marble were selected for construction of the new wings in place of the Virginia sandstone used in the old Capitol. The official cornerstone-laying for the new wings occurred on July 4, 1851, when President Millard Fillmore presided over the ceremony wearing the same Masonic apron that President Washington had used six decades earlier. But the real highlight of the day was the principal address delivered by old "Black Dan" himself, Daniel Webster. Webster, then Secretary of State, had spent most of the previous 30 years in the House and Senate. Against the background of worsening relations between the

In 1835, after attending the funeral for a Member of Congress, President Andrew Jackson was rushed on the steps of the Capitol by a would-be assassin. The President escaped death because both guns of the attacker misfired.

Robert Mills, architect of the Treasury Building and the Washington Monument, was an unsuccessful competitor for the 1850 extension project. This view of the Capitol shows his idea for a dome.

The old Supreme Court Chamber, restored in 1976.

Thomas U. Walter, the fourth Architect of the Capitol, was originally hired as the Architect of the extension. This 1851 elevation shows the proposed new House and Senate wings. The Bulfinch dome is still visible in this drawing.

Daniel Webster delivered a two-hour oration at the corner-stone laying ceremony for the extension in 1851.

Influence of classical architecture on U.S. Capitol. (L. to R.) St. Paul's Cathedral, London; U.S. Capitol; St. Peter's Cathedral, Rome; all drawn to same scale. The grandeur of the two cathedral domes undoubtedly influenced Thomas U. Walter's design for the dome of our Capitol.

North and South, Webster's speech became a plea for the preservation of the Union. Of the three former rhetorical "giants" of the Senate, Calhoun was dead, Clay was near the end of his brilliant career, and Webster was in the final year of his life.

If the future of the Republic seemed in doubt, that of the Capitol was not. Thomas Walter pressed ahead with the new Senate and House wings. By late 1857, the House of Representatives moved into its new Chamber, and in January of 1859, the Senate occupied the north wing, although much embellishment and dec-

orative work remained to be done. It had been apparent almost from the beginning of the expansion that, despite the intentional visual harmony of the new and old sections, the Bulfinch dome was dwarfed by the bulk of the enlarged Capitol. The decision was made to replace the dome with one more proportionate to the whole structure, one which was in fact nearly twice as high as the old Bulfinch dome. Walter drew on elements present in several of the great domes of the Old World—for example, St. Peter's in Rome and St. Paul's in London—to produce the masterpiece that today is instantly recognizable worldwide.

An allegorical female figure representing freedom was chosen to be placed atop the dome. In an early sketch, *Freedom* wore a liberty cap inspired by antique classical models and associated with freedom from slavery. Secretary of War Jefferson Davis objected to that symbolism from the Southern point of view that such a depiction would only further inflame the pro- and anti-slavery passions that were sweeping the country in the mid-19th century. Therefore, Thomas Crawford, the sculptor, altered his design, substituting a helmet surmounted by an eagle's head and feathers and encircled with stars.

Crawford's *Statue of Freedom* was fortunate to arrive in America at all. The sculptor modeled the statue in his studio in Rome. In April of 1858 his full-size plaster model was shipped from Leghorn, Italy, for casting in America. The boat carrying the statue was so old and slow that it took a full month to cross the Mediterranean, and even then was forced to put in at Gibraltar for the repair of her many leaks. After a month in Gibraltar, the ship sailed again for New York, and this time made it as far as Bermuda, where the leaks were judged so exten-

ST. PAUL'S U.S. CAPITOL ST. PETER'S

sive that the ship was pronounced a total loss and sold. It was not until December 1858, that *Freedom* arrived in New York, and it was to be another 5 years before she was cast in bronze and placed on the tholos of the Capitol dome.

The enlarged Capitol offered legislators a luxury of space on a scale that was not possible in the old building. Ample offices were provided for principal officers of both Houses, while comfortable lobbies were included for the relaxation of Senators and Representatives. Another innovation in 1859 was the installation of marble bathtubs. In the days when many Senators and Representatives lived in rooming houses and hotels that boasted few amenities, the handsome marble tubs, located in the Capitol basement, provided a popular service. Two remain, but they are in unusable condition in a basement area now used by Senate engineers.

During the 1850s the slavery debate became more intense and angry, thus confirming Daniel Webster's worst fears. Congress had always been "rough-and-tumble." Vice President Martin Van Buren had occasionally worn a brace of pistols thrust in his belt while presiding over the Senate. Tempers flared frequently, and a Senator from South Carolina wrote that "every man on the floor of both Houses is armed with a revolver." On May 20, 1856, Senator Charles Sumner of Massachusetts rose to denounce Senator A.P. Butler's stand on

This is a rare photograph of a detail of Thomas Crawford's *Freedom*. Designed in 1856, the statue was raised into place on top of the dome in 1863.

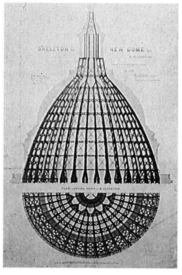

Drawn by Thomas U. Walter this study shows the skeletal arrangement of the dome's interior ironwork.

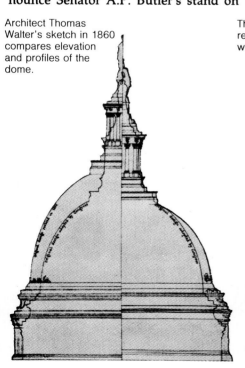

Architect Thomas Walter's sketch in 1860 compares elevation and profiles of the dome.

This cross-section rendering of the dome was prepared in 1859.

After extensive study the dome was constructed as shown in this drawing.

The Hall of Columns is located on the first floor of the House wing. The marble and bronze statues are part of the National Statuary Hall Collection.

The assault on Senator Sumner by a Member of the House of Representatives is depicted in this 1856 edition of Frank Leslie's Illustrated Newspaper.

the Kansas-Nebraska Act, which had repealed the Missouri Compromise and instead made it theoretically possible for the Nebraska Territory to enter the Union as a slave state. He characterized Senator Butler, an aging South Carolinian, as a Don Quixote who made vows to a mistress, "though polluted in the sight of the world, is chaste in his sight. I mean the harlot, slavery." Two days later, in the nearly empty Chamber, Sumner was approached at his desk by Representative Preston Brooks of South Carolina, a kinsman of Senator Butler. Brooks said, "I have read your speech twice over carefully; it is a libel on South Carolina, and Mr. Butler, who is a relative of mine." Without another word, Brooks began to beat Senator Sumner with his heavy, metal-capped walking stick. Brooks continued to strike the Massachusetts Senator until he fell unconscious. Sumner's injuries were so severe that it was several years before he could return to his duties.

The inevitable rupture came in 1861, when Senators and Representatives from States which had seceded resigned from Congress and left Washington. When the first influx of volunteers from the northeastern states began to pour into Washington, troops were billeted in the Capitol, since Congress was not in session at the time. A bakery was established in the basement committee rooms to feed the Union troops their daily 10-ounce bread ration. The committee rooms were turned over to the Army and stripped of all furniture and mantles. President Lincoln had originally asked for 75,000 volunteers willing to serve for 90 days, but it soon became apparent that the war would be a long and hard-fought struggle. The carefree young men who had camped out in the rotunda were molded into hardened soldiers by the time the Second Battle of Manassas and the Battle of

Antietam were fought in 1862. Thousands of wounded men from the two engagements spilled into Washington, filling the Army hospitals which had been established in public buildings. In the midst of the emergency the Capitol was again employed. Some 1,500 cots were set up in its great open spaces, and they were quickly filled with wounded soldiers.

Numerous anecdotes are preserved which reflect the intense emotions of this period. Early in the conflict a Union Army private at the Capitol was shown the Senate Chamber desk occupied by Senator Jefferson Davis in the years before the war. In an outburst of frustrated rage, he thrust his bayonet deeply into the dark mahogany desk. The damage has long since been skillfully repaired.

Throughout these trying months work on the great cast iron dome had gone ahead under Thomas Walter's direction. Colonel Montgomery Meigs, Chief of the Army Corps of Engineers, halted construction for a short time during the summer of 1861, but President Lincoln's personal determination to see the Capitol completed had prevailed. He was once asked by a visitor, John Eaton of Ohio, how he could justify the continued construction of the building, especially of the cast iron dome. Lincoln calmly replied that the work must continue. "If the people see the Capitol going on, it is a sign that we intend the Union shall go on." In late 1863 the President must have felt supremely vindicated. That year brought victories at Vicksburg and Gettysburg which pointed the way to ultimate triumph for the Union. On December 2, while Lincoln lay in bed with a fever, a huge crowd gathered in the Capitol Plaza to watch while the sections of Thomas Crawford's *Statue of Freedom* were raised to the summit of the dome and bolted together. Upon the completion of the task, a 35 gun salute was answered from the guns of the 12 surrounding forts that protected Washington.

During the Civil War the rotunda became a field hospital. Work on the dome was halted for a while but the elaborate scaffolding needed for its construction was left in place. Allyn Cox recorded this moment as part of the decorations for the House corridor (1974).

During the Civil War parts of the Capitol were used for the troops. In this view supplies are shown stored under the Senate Chamber while bread ovens were in rooms on the basement floor.

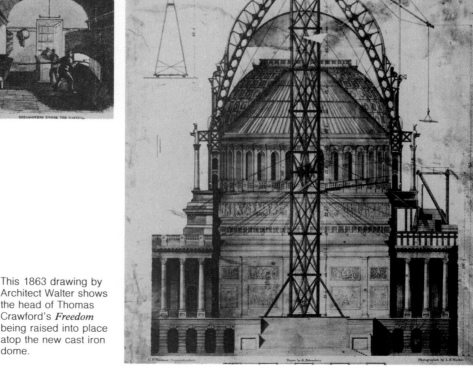

This 1863 drawing by Architect Walter shows the head of Thomas Crawford's *Freedom* being raised into place atop the new cast iron dome.

19

Stages of Growth and Restoration

House wing under construction. With the extension of the building it was necessary to remove the iron Bulfinch gates and enlarge the grounds. Three of the supporting square piers are now located on Constitution Avenue and 17th Street, Northwest.

The original Capitol was built of Aquia Creek sandstone from Virginia. The structure was 352 feet 4 inches in length at ground level and 282 feet 10½ inches in width including the east portico and steps. The Capitol has since more than doubled in length. The cost of this original building, including the grading of the grounds, was $2,432,851.34.

The old copper covered wooden dome was replaced by 1863 with the now familiar cast iron structure. The overall width of the dome at the base is 135 feet 5 inches. The rotunda, or interior of the dome, is 96 feet in diameter, and the height from the floor to the top of the canopy is 180 feet 3 inches. The Capitol has a floor area of 16½ acres, with 540 rooms devoted to offices, storage, restaurants and other purposes. There are 658 windows and 850 doorways. The dome receives light through 108 windows and there are 365 steps from the basement floor to the top of the dome.

Throughout the latter half of the 19th century, many improvements were made in the Capitol. Plumbing, steam heat, and forced air ventilation were introduced by 1865; the first elevators went into operation in 1874; the building was completely wired for electricity by 1900; and in 1901 the

Capitol was more adequately fire-proofed. As a byproduct of the modernization process, the Capitol did lose some of its romance; one by one its fireplaces were taken out of service. Only in recent years have some been made operable again.

In 1929, Congress authorized the installation of air-conditioning, then a radical innovation, in the Capitol and the House and Senate Buildings. When the Capitol Power Plant was expanded three years later, it held the largest air-conditioning unit in the world.

In 1935 the Supreme Court vacated its quarters in the old north wing of the Capitol and moved into its new marble building facing the Capitol. The room in which the Court had met from 1860—the original Senate Chamber—was stripped of its decoration and used as a general meeting room. The Law Library on the first floor was divided into three rooms and its splendid "umbrella" vault hidden by a dropped ceiling.

During the period from July 1949 to January 1951 the roofs and skylights of the Senate and House wings and the connecting corridors were replaced with new roofs of concrete and steel covered with copper.

New Senate wing nearly completed, the House wing and the dome still under construction. In May 1861 the Illustrated London News carried this woodcut. It was slightly in advance of the actual progress as the Senate steps and portico had not progresssed this far. Tiber Creek runs down the mall toward the half-completed Washington Monument.

The cast iron and glass ceilings of the Senate and House Chambers were replaced with new ceilings of stainless steel and plaster, and a laylight of carved glass and bronze was placed in the center of each ceiling. Alterations and improvements, lighting, and acoustics were made to the interiors of each Chamber, the cloakroom and adjacent areas. These alterations were the first major changes made in the Senate and House in the 90 years since their initial occupancy.

During the renovations, the Senate and House vacated their Chambers on three occasions to allow the work to progress. The Senate held its sessions in the old Senate Chamber and the House met in what is now the Ways and Means Committee Room in the Longworth House Office Building.

In 1956 Congress authorized the extension, reconstruction and replacement of the central portion of the Capitol and other related improvements. Under the approved plans, a new east front in marble from Georgia, faithfully reproducing the design of the old standstone front, was extended 32½ feet east of the old front. The east walls of the connecting corridors between the central front and the Senate and House wings were also extended in marble from Massachusetts (the marble for the columns came from Maryland). The old sandstone walls remained in place and became a part of the interior wall.

This work was begun in 1958 under the direction of the Architect of the Capitol and was completed in

Early photograph of the Capitol about 1850. Note the small cast iron balcony on the Senate side. A connecting corridor and the present Senate wing now obliterate this view of the original north wing.

By water to the Capitol in 1860. From the White House side or mall end this was the scene more than 100 years ago, showing the old canal and the Botanic Garden.

Horsecars at the Capitol (summer 1872). The horsecar line ran across the east plaza. Blocks of marble are visible in the foreground but construction is completed.

The Capitol, 1861. Less than a month after Lincoln's first inauguration the Civil War broke out and troops were called to protect the Capitol. Statuary for the Senate pediment and troops drilling on the east lawn were all part of the Capitol scene this May day of 1861.

1962. Additional work included repairs to the dome, construction of a subway terminal under the Senate wing steps and reconstruction of the steps, cleaning of the Senate and House wings, birdproofing the building, furniture and furnishings for the new areas, and improved lighting throughout the building.

Since the 1970's work on the Capitol has emphasized a higher standard of maintenance and a renewed appreciation for the building's architectural history. In anticipation of the Nation's Bicentennial, the old Senate Chamber and the original Supreme Court Chamber were restored to their mid-nineteenth century appearance. National Stautory Hall, formerly the old House Chamber before 1864, also was restored. This work included draping the colonnade, reproducing the historic lighting fixtures and repainting.

The restoration of the west central front, the most ambitious restoration project in the history of the Capitol, was begun in 1983 and completed in 1987. It is the only elevation of the old Capitol that has not been covered by marble additions. The restoration of the west central front first required the removal of multiple layers of paint

The plaster model of *Hope Protecting Genius,* the first figure of the House pediment is hoisted into position. The completed grouping is known as *The Apotheosis of Democracy,* and the original models may be seen in the Capitol terminal of the Rayburn subway.

Pediment of the House wing nears completion. The sculptural work by Paul W. Bartlett was authorized in 1908 and the unveiling ceremony took place in 1916. Here craftsmen are about to put another allegorical figure into position.

which had been applied to the sandstone since 1818 as weatherproofing. To return the deteriorated west front to a pristine condition, approximately 40 percent of the Aquia Creek sandstone was removed and replaced with Indiana limestone. The stone replacement was preceded by a careful analysis of each stone's structural stability. Stainless steel tie rods were drilled into the walls to reinforce the vaulted structure. All windows were replaced to increase energy efficiency. After a consolidant was applied to strengthen the stone, the west front was repainted and the restoration work completed.

A marble monolithic column for the Senate portico is swung into place. In the background the dome nears completion.

During the extension of the east front between 1958 and 1962, the original sandstone portico was removed. It was replicated in marble in front of the 32 feet of added space.

The original House
of Representatives
Chamber was restored
to some of its 1822
splendor during 1976.
The Chamber became
Statuary Hall in 1864.

The old Supreme Court
Chamber was restored
to include
reproductions of
furnishings used in the
Chamber in the 1800s.
This project, directed
by George M. White,
Architect of the Capitol,
was completed in
1976.

Restoration of the old Senate Chamber was completed in June of 1976 under the supervision of the Senate Commission on Art and Antiquities. The mid-19th-century furnishings remind one of the days of the eloquence of Webster, Clay, and Calhoun.

The United States Senate, A.D. 1850, engraved by Robert Whitechurch after Peter Rothermel. Henry Clay presents his program of compromise in the old Senate Chamber, presided over by Vice President Millard Fillmore. John C. Calhoun appears to the right of the Vice President and Daniel Webster is seated left foreground, head in hand.

Second floor passageway before reconstruction. The passage was constructed in 1901. At that time, the walls were covered in white glazed brick.

Second floor passageway after modification. Caen stone walls, octagonal marble floor, ornamental plaster ceiling and appropriate chandelier embellish the space.

Originally, a grand staircase occupied this space. After the fire of 1814, Latrobe abandoned that design and constructed a small rotunda inside the existing oval space.

The west front of the Capitol was covered with scaffold and flanked with two cranes during its restoration between 1983 and 1987.

Repairs to sidewalk on the east front of Capitol.

Art in the Capitol

The Capitol is a recognized work of art. The classical architecture and the interior embellishments, from Benjamin Latrobe's unique corncob and tobacco capitals to Constantino Brumidi's powerful dome fresco, set the backdrop for the variety and scope of American history and culture.

Since 1872, the Joint Committee on the Library has had supervision of all works of art in the Capitol and is authorized to accept any work of fine art on behalf of the Congress. Much of the collection is catalogued in a book entitled: *Art in the Capitol*, published by the Architect of the Capitol

Brumidi's canopy and fresco frieze complement the classical cast iron details of Thomas Walter's dome. A bronze replica of Houdon's statue of George Washington stands in the foreground.

Benjamin Latrobe designed the corncob capitals for the columns in the foyer outside the old Supreme Court Chamber (1809).

Some of Brumidi's most beautiful room paintings are found in S–127, the Senate Committee on Appropriations' room. Pompeian architecture and allegorical figures dominate the compositions on all the walls and ceiling.

On the first floor
Senate corridor
Brumidi painted walls
and ceilings with
medallion portraits,
sketches of major
inventions, and
paintings of birds,
animals and flowers.

The ceiling in the
President's Room is
ornately decorated.
This allegoric female
figure is reminiscent of
earlier Italian paintings
of Madonnas.

The President's Room, with frescos and oil paintings, dates to about 1860. Until the 1930's, Presidents signed bills at the mahogany table under the great crystal and bronze chandelier.

under the direction of the Joint Committee on the Library.

Sculpture is the earliest form of art in the Capitol, designed both to complement the classical style of the building and to add symbolic meaning. Because there were no sculptors in America, they were brought to the Capitol from Europe. Two notable examples of such artists and their work are Carlo Franzoni's relief of *Justice,* created for the Supreme Court Chamber, and the majestic *Liberty and the Eagle* by Enrico Causici, created for the old House Chamber.

Paintings of historical subjects were first commissioned from John Trumbull, who had designed eight Revolutionary scenes to fit the framed niches on the walls of the rotunda. Congress, however, commissioned only four of these paintings in 1817,

First Reading of the Emancipation Proclamation, by Francis B. Carpenter, in the west staircase of the Senate wing. Lincoln is shown with his cabinet. Seated: Edwin M. Stanton, President Lincoln, Gideon Welles, William H. Seward, Edward Bates; standing: Salmon P. Chase, Caleb B. Smith, Montgomery Blair.

and later chose other artists to fill the four remaining niches.

Portraits in oil, bronze, and marble constitute a large portion of the art collection, including a portrait of General Lafayette which was given to the House of Representatives by artist Ary Scheffer in commemoration of Lafayette's return visit to Washington, D.C. in 1824.

The construction of the new House and Senate wings and the cast iron dome in the 1850's and 1860's provided many opportunities for adding works of art to the Capitol. Three sets of doors cast in bronze were installed in the Capitol. The first set, depicting events in the life of Christopher Columbus, was designed by Randolf Rogers in Rome, Italy. The remaining two, depicting American Revolutionary events, were designed by Thomas Crawford, also in Rome. Other notable works designed by Crawford include the *Statue of Freedom* atop the dome, the Senate pediment *Progress of Civilization,* and the statues of *Justice* and *History* located above the Senate bronze doors, east portico.

Although much remained to be finished in the wings, the House of Representatives first met in its new Chamber on December 16, 1857, and the Senate met in its new Chamber on January 4, 1859. Once both Houses of Congress vacated their rooms in the old Capitol, it became necessary to

Washington at Valley Forge, 1778 is on the south wall of the Senate Appropriations Room.

find a use for each of those historic Chambers.

The old Senate Chamber was easily converted for use by the Supreme Court. The original House Chamber was another matter: it was too large to be used for any subsidiary function, too handsome a room to subdivide into office space, and traffic between the House and Senate wings passed directly through it. After 1857 the House almost seemed to forget its existence, and the Chamber fell into disuse and disrepair. Old furniture, boxes, and other unwanted material were stored in its corners.

In 1864, Representative Justin Morrill of Vermont rose in the House to offer a solution to the dilemma: "To what end more useful or grand, and at the same time simple and inexpensive, can we devote it (the old Chamber) than to ordain that it shall be set apart for the reception of such statuary as each State shall elect to be deserving of this lasting commemoration?" His proposal became law on July 2, 1864, thus creating National Statuary Hall. Rhode Island's Quaker General, Nathanael Greene, was the first person to be honored.

By the early 1930s, 65 statues were crowded into Statuary Hall. In some places they were lined three deep, and engineers discovered that their excessive weight was endangering the structure of the floor, as the

Hall was in one of the oldest parts of the building. In 1933, and again in 1976, Congress provided for the relocation of many of these statues to other areas in the Capitol, and those remaining were arranged in a more attractive pattern. All but six States have contributed both of their statues to the collection.

During the partial restoration of Statuary Hall for the 1976 Bicentennial, the coffered half-dome ceiling was decorated, the walls and columns were cleaned, and replicas of the original brass chandelier and sconces were

installed. Heavy scarlet brocade draperies, reproductions of the originals, were hung in the old visitors' gallery. Duplicates of the early fireplace mantels were placed at the reopened fireplaces.

The rich interior decoration of the new wings, reflecting the Victorian taste of the time, contrasts with the relatively plain sandstone and plaster walls of the old Capitol. Door and window frames, made of fire-proof cast iron, were molded into decorative borders. Many of the rooms retain their original ornate gilded mirrors.

The Declaration of Independence by John Trumbull, one of the eight paintings in the rotunda, depicts a monumental event in our history. In Independence Hall, Philadelphia, July 4, 1776, 56 signers, all Members of the Continental Congress, risked death to tell the world that "for the support of this Declaration . . . we mutually pledge to each other our Lives, our Fortunes, and our sacred Honor."

Calling of Putnam From the Plow to the Revolution by Constantino Brumidi, is on the west wall of the House Appropriations Room. Putnam left his farm to fight in the Battle of Breed's Hill, June 16, 1775. It was the first fresco in the Capitol.

The floors are covered with encaustic tiles in hundreds of different patterns and a rich range of color. These tiles were manufactured by the Minton Company of England. Each wing has two massive stairways of marble and two private staircases with beautifully detailed bronze railings.

Three major fires in the Capitol have caused the destruction of works of art. During the War of 1812 the British burned the Capitol on August 24, 1814. Furniture was piled in the House and Senate Chambers and then "put to the torch." The Library of Congress (in the Capitol from 1800 to 1897) was almost totally destroyed by an accidental fire on December 24, 1851. Over three-fifths of the books were burned and many paintings, portraits and busts were lost. A fire on January 3, 1930, in an attic room where models were made and stored, caused some additional losses.

Constantino Brumidi, born in Rome, Italy in 1805, is sometimes called the "Michelangelo of the Capitol" because he contributed so much to the decoration of the Capitol extensions and dome. His murals, portraits, lunettes, and frescos are representative of his wide range of artistic skills. He emigrated to the United States in 1852 and eventually became a citizen. Bru-

midi was hired in 1855 by the Superintendent of the Capitol, Montgomery Meigs, to decorate the Agriculture Committee Room in the Capitol, thus providing the first example of fresco in America. His work was so well received that he continued as the artist of the Capitol for the next 25 years. His legacy includes the corridors of the Senate wing, the President's Room, the Senate Reception Room and the present House and Senate Appropriations Committee Rooms. For the corridors he painted frescoed lunettes and medallion portraits. Brumidi left spaces blank to allow for representation of important events in the future. Later artists added landscapes, the Wright Brothers' airplane, and, most recently, the *First Moon Landing* and a tribute to the *Challenger* crew.

Brumidi's most impressive work is the canopy fresco covering 4,664 square feet over the eye of the dome in the rotunda, 180 feet above the floor. The fresco depicts *The Apotheosis of George Washington.* Flanked by Liberty and Victory, the deified President rises to the heavens, encircled by 13 maidens representing the original States. Six groups around the perimeter combine classical gods with important figures in American history. Brumidi's last work was the frescoed frieze encircling the rotunda 58 feet above the floor. Starting with figures of *America in History,* Brumidi chose 15 epic events in American history from the *Landing of Columbus, 1492,* to the *Discovery of Gold in California, 1848.* While working on *Penn's Treaty With the Indians,* the 74-year-old artist slipped on his scaffold, where he clung for nearly 20 minutes until rescued. The shock of the accident severely weakened him, and he died a few months later in 1880, with only one-third of the frieze completed. His designs were carried out by Filippo Costaggini, also Italian-born and trained. A 32-foot gap that remained was finally filled with three scenes by Allyn Cox in 1953. Brumidi's great wish, which he once expressed in a letter, was "that I may live long enough to make beautiful the Capitol of the one country on earth in which there is liberty."

In 1987 conservator Bernard Rabin and his staff began restoration on the canopy fresco, which had darkened with dirt and grime and had been overpainted in many areas. The task was completed in June 1988. The frieze of the rotunda was restored in

George Washington by Rembrandt Peale. This distinguished portrait is known because of its illusionistically painted frame as the "porthole portrait." Purchased for the Senate in 1832, it hangs in the old Senate Chamber.

"C. Brumidi, Artist, Citizen of the U.S." is how Brumidi signed *Cornwallis Sues for Cessation of Hostilities*

Under the Flag of Truce. The fresco is located in the House Dining Room.

The Columbus Doors, designed by Randolph Rogers, originally hung in the corridor connecting Statuary Hall with the House wing. In 1871 they were moved to the east front entrance.

Diagram of bronze doors of the main entrance to the rotunda—east front, U.S. Capitol.

BUST OF COLUMBUS

EAGLE AND FLAGS

LANDING OF COLUMBUS IN THE NEW WORLD
OCT. 12, 1492

ASIA	VESPUCCI	① DEPARTURE OF COLUMBUS FROM PALOS	MENDOZA	ALEXANDER VI	② COLUMBUS' FIRST ENCOUNTER WITH THE INDIANS	PIZARRO	AFRICA
	OJEDA	③ AUDIENCE AT THE COURT OF FERDINAND AND ISABELLA	ISABELLA	FERDINAND	④ ENTRY OF COLUMBUS INTO BARCELONA	BALBOA	
	CORTEZ	⑤ COLUMBUS' DEPARTURE FROM THE CONVENT OF LA RABIDA	BOBADILLA	CHARLES VIII	⑥ COLUMBUS IN CHAINS	B. COLUMBUS	
EUROPE	PEREZ	⑦ COLUMBUS BEFORE THE COUNCIL OF SALAMANCA	HENRY VII	JOHN II	⑧ DEATH OF COLUMBUS	PINZON	AMERICA

1986 by Rabin. The sculpted bronze stair railings of the Members' staircases, designed by Brumidi, also have been cleaned and restored.

Through the efforts of Mrs. Myrtle G. Murdock, who published the only book on the artist, Brumidi's grave was located in the District of Columbia's Glenwood Cemetery for which Congress provided a bronze marker in 1950. On April 30, 1968, the Brumidi bust, sculpted by Virginia artist, Miss Jimilu Mason, was dedicated in a ceremony in the rotunda. Representative Frank Annunzio and Senator Paul Douglas, both of Illinois, sponsored legislation passed by Congress which authorized that the bust of Brumidi be placed in a permanent place of honor in the corridor, known as Brumidi Corridor, on the first floor of the Senate wing of the Capitol.

Major works added by other artists in the late 19th century include Emmanuel Leutze's *Westward the Course of Empire Takes Its Way,* and two landscapes by Albert Bierstadt, *Discovery of the Hudson River* and *Entrance Into Monterey.* The pace of commissioning and accepting works of art has slowed in the 20th century for lack of space. In 1905, H. Lyman Sayen installed four lunettes stretched on canvas for the Committee on Insular Affairs. The boldness of their outlines and color has been revealed by recent cleaning and restoration. Howard Chandler Christy's *Scene of the Signing of the Constitution* was authorized by Congress in 1939 after much debate over the

Scene at the Signing of the Constitution, by Howard Chandler Christy, was painted in 1940 and placed in the east stairway of the House wing. This 20 x 30 foot canvas, largest in the Capitol, is remarkable for its historic detail and its patriotic inspiration. Eleven years after independence was declared, the leaders of the new Nation met in Independence Hall, September 17, 1787, to place their names on this modern document of freedom. Well-known likenesses of George Washington, Benjamin Franklin, Alexander Hamilton and James Madison are easily recognized.

wisdom of spending funds for art during the Depression. It stands today as the only representation of all the signers and was frequently reproduced during the celebration of the Bicentennial of the Constitution. Two corridors on the first floor of the House were filled with scenes from American history by Allyn Cox between 1973 and 1985, and a third corridor, based on his designs, is scheduled to be painted.

This detail of Freedom triumphing over Tyranny and Kingly Power reveals the beauty of the recently cleaned fresco.

Conservator Bernard Rabin discusses restoration of Brumidi's *Apotheosis of George Washington* with Chairman Annunizo and Vice Chairman Ford of the Joint Committee on Printing and George M. White, Architect of the Capitol.

The central area of *The Apotheosis of George Washington* shows the face of the President after the removal of grime and overpaint. The area to the left is uncleaned, while the upper quadrant has received preliminary cleaning.

Gods and mortals mingle in the dome's fresco. (1) Armed Freedom—Brumidi's young wife was the model—triumphs over Tyranny and Kingly Power. (2) Ceres rides a reaper as Young America, wearing a liberty cap, stands near.

(3) Vulcan rests his foot on a cannon. (4) Sandaled Mercury offers a bag of gold to Robert Morris.

(5) Bearded Neptune and Aphrodite, holding the Atlantic cable, rise from the sea. (6) Wise Minerva speaks to Benjamin Franklin, S.F.B. Morse, and Robert Fulton.

(1) America in History.
(2) Landing of Columbus, 1492. (3) Entry of Cortez into the Halls of Montezuma, 1521. (4) Pizarro's Conquest of Peru, 1533. (5) Midnight Burial of De Soto in the Mississippi, 1542.

1   2   3

(6) Pocahontas Saving Life of Capt. John Smith, 1607. (7) Landing of Pilgrims at Plymouth, Mass., 1620. (8) Penn's Treaty With the Indians, 1682. (9) Colonization of New England. (10) Peace between Governor Oglethorpe and the Indians, 1732.

6   7

(11) Battle of Lexington, 1775. (12) Reading of the Declaration of Independence, 1776. (13) Surrender of Cornwallis at Yorktown, 1781. (14) Death of Tecumseh at Battle of Thames, 1813.

11   12

(15) Entry of General Scott into the City of Mexico, 1847. (16) Discovery of Gold in California, 1848. (17) The Civil War, 1865. (18) The Spanish-American War, 1898. (19) Birth of Aviation in the United States, 1903.

15   16

4   5

8   9   10

13   14

17   18   19

The House Reading Room, is dominated by its Minton tile floors, designed to resemble oriental rugs. This room, convenient to the House floor, provides Members with their local newspapers. The cherubic bronze wall sconces are the oldest original Capitol lighting fixtures in use.

The Speaker's Lobby
is flanked with portraits
of former Speakers.
The carpet that runs
the length of the lobby
was woven to resemble
the Minton tile in the
adjoining Reading
Room.

Baluster and Rails of
bronze were designed
by Constantino
Brumidi, in 1857. Two
stairways in the Senate
wing and two in the
House are decorated
with these bronze
designs.

The Senate Reception Room features a series of portraits of five former U.S. Senators selected as outstanding among those who served in the U.S. Senate before 1959.

America's First Moon Landing, 1969 was inserted in an oval in the Brumidi corridor by Allyn Cox in 1975. Apollo blasting off is shown in the lower section, while above Astronauts Armstrong and Aldrin plant the American flag in front of the lunar module.

In April of 1955 the 83rd Congress opened a room for meditation for the Members of Congress, designed to be acceptable as a place of worship for any religion. The idea came jointly from former Senator A.S. "Mike" Monroney of Oklahoma, and former Representative Brooks Hays of Kansas. They introduced concurrent resolutions to set aside a place where the legislators might pray or meditate. Former Speaker Joseph W. Martin, Jr. of Massachusetts selected the location from space allocated for his personal use.

The window, which was an anonymous gift, is the focal point of this small, private room. The seal of the United States, a biblical quotation, and the names of the fifty States surround the central figure of George Washington kneeling.

A mural honoring the crew of the Space Shuttle *Challenger,* is displayed in the Brumidi corridor of the Senate wing. The mural, unveiled on March 3, 1987, was painted by artist Charles Schmidt of Temple University.

Junipero Serra, 1713–1784, California, Ettore Cadorin, 1930, bronze, 8′9″, Statuary Hall.

George Washington, 1732–1799, Virginia Antoine Houdon, bronze, 7′6″, 1909 casting from the original 1788 marble Capitol rotunda.

Landing of Columbus at the Island of Guanahani, West Indies, *October 12th, 1492,* John Vanderlyn, 12′x18′, Capitol rotunda.

Benjamin Franklin,
1706–1790, H. Powers,
1862; marble 7´11˝,
Senate wing, second
floor, east corridor.

Martin Luther King, Jr.,
Georgia
John Wilson
House wing, first floor.

*Embarkation of the
Pilgrims at Delft Haven,
Holland, July 22nd,*
1620, Robert W. Weir,
1843; 12´x18´, Capitol
rotunda.

Andrew Jackson, 1767–1845, Tennessee, Belle Kinney Scholz, New York, 1927, bronze 7'6", Capitol rotunda.

Brighman Young, 1801–1877, Utah, Mahonri Young, marble, 5'11", Statuary Hall.

Will Rogers, 1879–1935, Oklahoma, Jo Davidson, Paris, 1938, bronze, 7'6" House connecting corridor.

Pocahontas, unknown artist, copy from original, 30"x25", S–233, The Capitol.

Ætatis suæ 21. Aº. 1616.

Matoaks als Rebecka daughter to the mighty Prince
Powhatan Emperour of Attanoughkomouck als Virginia
converted and baptized in the Christian faith, and
wife to the worfh. Mr Tho: Rolff.

Battle of Lake Erie,
William H. Powell,
20'x30', Senate wing,
east staircase.

*Electoral Commission of
1877 (Florida Case),*
Cornelia A. Fassett,
1879, 61½"x75",
Senate wing, third
floor, east corridor.

Discovery of the Hudson River, Albert Bierstadt, 6′x10′, Members' private stairway, east corridor.

Thomas Jefferson, Thomas Sully, 29½″x24½″, S–210, The Capitol.

Patrick Henry, George B. Matthews, after Thomas Sully, 29½″x24½″, Senate wing, second floor, main corridor.

Niagara Falls in Winter, Regis Gignoux, 1848, 52"x36", Senate wing, third floor, south corridor.

King Kamehameha I. Hawaii, 1758–1819, Thomas R. Gould, bronze, 8'7", Statuary Hall.

Indian Fountain, William H. Rinehart, bronze, 1857, SB–14, The Capitol.

The Capitol Guide Service.

Staircase on the east side of the Senate wing.

The people who visit the Capitol of the United States come for many reasons and from a multitude of backgrounds. The Nation's citizens visit the Capitol with feelings of ownership, pride and unity; they come to see the place where the President is inaugurated, to see the workings of their Government, to meet their representatives, to show their children the national heritage. And from around the world, millions come each year to see one of the greatest living symbols of freedom and self-government.

Before these visitors, the Capitol spreads a story, depicted alike in paintings, sculpture, architecture and daily business—the struggle of a people to govern themselves, to be and to remain free.

It is vital to our form of Government that the people be able to see and hear the machinery of legislation in motion. In the House and Senate Chambers, visitors watch from galleries while the Members of Congress debate the issues of Government.

The people also speak. Many come to seek counsel with their Representatives or Senators. They may need help, or wish to make known their position on matters of legislation.

Perhaps the most important visitors are the students, the young people of the world who visit the Capitol and see its workings, its spirit and its substance. Many have studied the forms and history of U.S. Government, but without these visits they can have little idea of the vast range of activities behind the final acts of legislation.

It is an "open" Capitol. Visitors roam the halls and grounds of the Capitol Hill complex at their leisure. Tours and signs and guidebooks are offered to increase the value of their visiting time.

Groups or individuals may request admittance to the House and Senate Galleries from their Representative or Senator. The Member writes a letter to the proper official, requesting that the group be admitted, with a copy of the letter to the group leader, who shows it to the Doorkeeper.

Individuals may also obtain passes for admission to the House Gallery from a Representative; admission to the Senate Gallery is gained by a pass issued by a Senator. The two passes are not interchangeable, and they do not admit the bearer to special events and to a joint session of the Congress. House Gallery passes are good for both sessions of Congress. Senate Gallery passes are good for only one session.

One organization is authorized by Congress to provide tours, at no charge, through the interior of the U.S. Capitol.

The original Guide Service was established in 1876 as an outgrowth of the Philadelphia Centennial and the

One of the stops on the tour is a Brumidi corridor.

resultant increased volume of visitors to the U.S. Capitol Building. Guides were unsalaried employees appointed by the Congress who derived their income from the 25-cent fee that was charged for the tour. This system remained in effect until January 3, 1971, when Title IV, Part 4 of Public Law 91–510 ". . . established an organization under the Congress of the United States, to be designated the 'Capitol Guide Service' . . .".

Jurisdiction over the Capitol Guide Service was vested in the Committee on Rules and Administration of

This view of the small Senate rotunda shows the Latrobe tobacco leaf capitals and a 19th century chandelier.

Bust of Abraham Lincoln by Gutzon Borglum is located in the crypt.

A reflecting visitor in the Capitol rotunda.

the Senate and the Committee on House Administration of the House of Representatives. The Capitol Guide Board, composed of the two Sergeants at Arms and the Architect of the Capitol, was created to direct, supervise and control the Capitol Guide Service.

Public tours of the Capitol Building are offered between 9:00 a.m. and 3:45 p.m., 7 days a week except for Thanksgiving, Christmas and New Year's Day. Tours begin at least every 15 minutes and during the busy season as frequently as every 2 minutes. They cover as many points of interest as possible coincident with existing conditions within the Capitol Building. Over 67 percent of the visitors to the Capitol visit during the 5 months of April through August of each year.

There are many works of art in the rotunda to interest visitors.

The size of the rotunda paintings and sculpted reliefs reflects the grand scale of this area.

A tourist records his visit to the Capitol.

A Capitol guide leads a tour.

The famous "whispering spot" in Statuary Hall.

Architects of the Capitol

Responsibilities of the Architect of the Capitol

The first Architect of the Capitol was appointed in 1793 by President George Washington. During the period of construction of the Capitol (1793–1865) appointments were made to this position for various stages of the construction work required. However, the Office of the Architect has been continuously occupied since 1851.

William Thornton

Won the competition for designing the United States Capitol in 1793. As Architect supervised the beginning construction of the original North or Senate wing. Appointed as one of three District Commissioners, he continued supervising construction of the Capitol. Superintendents during this period were Stephen Hallet, James Hoban and George Hadfield.

The functions of this office have changed over the years in accordance with the increased activities imposed upon it by Congress, due principally to the addition of new buildings and grounds. Originally, the duties of the Architect were to plan and construct the Capitol Building, and later, to supervise its care and maintenance.

Although appointment to the office is made by the President, the Architect is a part of the Legislative Branch and serves as an agent of the Congress. In this capacity, he is charged with the planning, design and

Benjamin Henry Latrobe

Constructed the original House wing and remodeled the interior of the original Senate wing; after the fire of 1814 he redesigned and constructed the interiors of both wings, now Statuary Hall and the old Senate Chamber.

Born May 20, 1759, Jost van Dyke, West Indies. Died March 28, 1828, Washington, D.C. Appointed by President George Washington, 1793. Resigned September 12, 1794.

Born May 1, 1764, England. Died September 3, 1820, New Orleans, Louisiana. Appointed by President Thomas Jefferson, March 6, 1803—resigned July 1, 1811. Appointed by President James Madison, April 6, 1815—resigned November 20, 1817.

construction of buildings committed to his care by Congress.

The Architect is also charged with a broad range of construction, maintenance and management responsibilities that encompass the Capitol complex, including the Library of Congress Buildings, the Supreme Court Building, the U.S. Botanic Garden, the House and Senate Office Buildings, and the Capitol Power Plant. The Architect is responsible for maintenance and improvements of the Capitol grounds, comprising approximately 209 acres of landscaping, parks, streets, and parking.

Charles Bulfinch

One of the first American born architects of distinction. Constructed the center section and the original low wooden dome of the Capitol. His design also extended the west front from that planned by Latrobe. He planned the landscaping and the original earthen west terraces.

Born August 8, 1763, Boston, Mass. Died April 15, 1844, Boston, Mass. Appointed by President James Monroe, January 8, 1818. Office abolished June 25, 1829.

The activities of the Architect primarily fall under the direction and general policy of the Senate Committee on Rules and Administration, the Committee on House Administration and the House Office Building Commission. Under the direction of the Joint Committee on the Library, the Architect serves as Acting Director of the U.S. Botanic Garden.

Thomas Ustick Walter

Won the competition for the design to extend the wings of the Capitol and executed this work; was architect for the present high, iron dome; reconstructed interior of west center building to provide for the Library of Congress after the fire of 1851. Made first studies for extending the east and west central fronts of the Capitol.

Born September 4, 1804, Philadelphia, Pa. Died October 30, 1887, Philadelphia, Pa. Appointed by President Millard Fillmore, June 11, 1851. Resigned May 26, 1865.

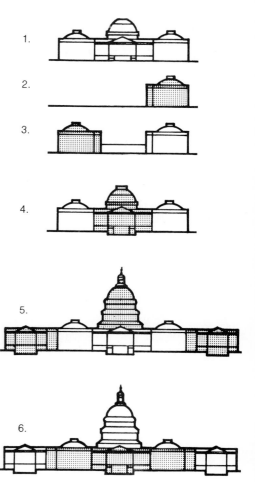

1. Original design by William Thornton, who won $500 in the competition held by the Commissioners of the newly-formed District of Columbia. The plan was approved by President George Washington in 1793.

2. North wing, occupied by the Congress in 1800.

3. South wing, completed by Benjamin Latrobe. A wooden passage connected the wings. Latrobe later restored the building after the fire of 1814, set by the invading British Army.

4. The central section of the Capitol was completed by Charles Bulfinch, whose construction of a low wooden dome was accomplished in 1829. Renovations abated until 1851, when construction of House and Senate extensions and a new, higher dome was begun.

5. Additions supervised by Thomas U. Walter. Work on the renovations continued from 1851 until the dome was completed in 1863.

6. Extension to the east central front of the Capitol was completed by J. George Stewart in 1962.

Edward Clark

Oversaw completion of the porticoes of the new wings; reconstructed the old Hall of Representatives for use as Statuary Hall; extended Capitol grounds and built present granite terraces; reconstructed and repaired old Supreme Court section after explosion and fire of 1898; replaced gas with electricity; reconstructed west central floors vacated by Library of Congress when it moved to its present building in 1897; supervised installation of elevators, fireproofing, incandescent lights, modernized heating and ventilation.

Born August 15, 1822, Philadelphia, Pennsylvania. Died January 6, 1902, Washington, D.C. Appointed by President Andrew Johnson, August 30, 1865. Died in office.

Elliott Woods

Oversaw the erection of the first House and Senate Office Buildings and subways; built the Capitol Power Plant; added 5th floor to Cannon House Office Building; built 28 rooms in the space formerly occupied by the Library of Congress in the Capitol; made significant changes in lighting, heating and ventilation.

Born February 2, 1865 near Manchester, England. Died May 22, 1923, Spring Lake, New Jersey. Appointed by President Theodore Roosevelt, February 19, 1902. Died in office.

David Lynn

Responsible for construction of the Longworth House Office Building; U.S. Supreme Court Building; Library of Congress Annex; First Street wing of the Russell Senate Office Building; built the Senate garage and expanded the Capitol grounds; added to the power plant; remodeled the Senate and House Chambers; constructed the Botanic Garden Conservatory; and began construction of the Dirksen Senate Office Building.

Born November 10, 1873, Wheeling, West Virginia. Died May 25, 1961, Washington, D.C. Appointed by President Calvin Coolidge, August 22, 1923, Retired September 30, 1954.

Thomas U. Walter's plan (1865) for the extension of the east front of the Capitol was realized about 100 years later. The Architect of the Capitol, J. George Stewart, directed this complex project.

J. George Stewart

Continued the work of his predecessor in construction of Dirksen Senate Office Building and connecting subways; continued improvements and expansion of the power plant; approved plans for Taft Memorial and bell tower; prepared the Prayer Room for Congressional use; extended east central front of the Capitol and rehabilitated the dome; responsible for construction of Rayburn House Office Building, connecting subway and the House underground garages; remodeled Cannon House Office Building and prepared plans for full remodeling of Longworth House Office Building; initiated improved interior and exterior lighting of the Capitol; responsible for preliminary plans for the James Madison Memorial Library of Congress Building and extension of the west central front of the Capitol.

Conservator Bernard Rabin consults with Architect of the Capitol, George M. White, during the cleaning of the Brumidi fresco in the dome of the Capitol.

Born June 2, 1890, Wilmington, Delaware. Died May 24, 1970, Washington, D.C. Appointed by President Dwight D. Eisenhower October 1, 1954. Died in office.

George Malcolm White

Responsible for construction of the James Madison Memorial Library of Congress Building; restoration of the old Supreme Court and old Senate Chambers in the Capitol; design of the extension to the Dirksen Senate Office Building; expansion program for the Capitol Power Plant; master plan for Capitol Hill; construction and equipment of the Philip A. Hart Senate Office Building; acquisition of additional property as part of Capitol grounds; House Office Building improvements; restoration of the west front of the Capitol and interior renovations; modification of the Thomas Jefferson and John Adams Buildings of the Library of Congress.

Born November 1, 1920, Cleveland, Ohio. Appointed by President Richard M. Nixon, January 27, 1971.

House and Senate Office Buildings

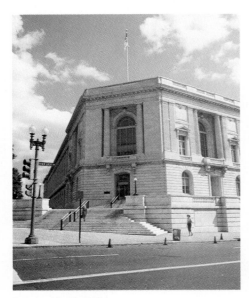

Cannon House Office Building.

Early in the twentieth century, two office buildings were constructed on the summit of Capitol Hill, one for each House. The Capitol had become overcrowded, and the two new structures were needed to accommodate a Congress grown to four hundred and thirty-five Representatives and ninety-six Senators. Space for committee hearings, files and documents was becoming limited by the size of the membership.

The new House office building, later named for the late Speaker Joseph Cannon of Illinois, was completed in 1908. The counterpart Senate office building, named for the late Senator Richard Russell of Georgia, was finished in 1909. John Carrere and Thomas Hastings designed both buildings as identical four-sided structures and their plans included a Caucus Room for each building.

Two additional House office buildings, named for the late Speakers Nicholas Longworth of Ohio and Sam Rayburn of Texas, as well as two buildings for the Senate, named for the late Senators Everett Dirksen of Illinois, and Philip Hart of Michigan, have also been constructed to accommodate the increasing demands for space by the Congress. Offices for Members and committees are located in the six office buildings adjacent to the Capitol. The day-to-day activities of the Members' offices and most committee meetings are conducted in these buildings.

The Caucus Room of the Russell Senate Office Building is one of the most historic rooms. The room was originally intended for political party caucuses or meetings where members of the same party decided upon their leadership, policies, and legislative matters. Prior to completion of the office building, each party held its meetings in locations in the Capitol such as the Senate Chamber and the Senate Reception Room.

The size and stateliness of the Caucus Room in the Russell Senate Office Building make it a frequent location for major public hearings where for the past three quarters of a centu-

Longworth House Office Building.

Rayburn House Office Building.

Russell Senate Office Building.

ry it has served as a stage for some of the most dramatic Senate investigations, such as the sinking of the *Titanic*, the Teapot Dome Scandal, Pearl Harbor, the Kefauver Crime Committee, the Army *vs.* McCarthy, the Vietnam-Era Conflict, Watergate, Judge Claiborne's impeachment trial, Judge Bork's nomination to the Supreme Court, and also, the Iran-Contra hearings.

The Caucus Room in the Cannon House Office Building is a grand and richly detailed room providing a dignified environment in which important political meetings and social functions are held. It is the oldest and one of the largest assembly rooms built for the House of Representatives outside the Capitol. Prior to the construction of the Cannon House Office Building, caucuses and other meetings took place in cramped committee rooms located in the Capitol.

The Congress has placed works of art throughout all the buildings in the Capitol complex. The Rayburn House Office Building displays a statue of the dynamic Speaker of the House from Texas, Sam Rayburn. The tunnel between the Cannon House Office Building and the Capitol is the site for a display of paintings done by high school artists, who enter their works in congressional district competitions sponsored by the Arts Caucus. The basement rotunda in the Cannon House Office Building displays a large model of the Capitol.

One of the newest and most impressive additions of art for a Senate Office Building is the Alexander Calder sculpture *Mountains and Clouds.* Designed for the Philip A. Hart Senate Office Building atrium in 1976 and installed in 1986, the imposing black structure combines a mobile and stabile, filling the entire courtyard space.

Particularly impressive is the mobile of four massive clouds that rotate slowly above.

Former Senator Nicholas F. Brady of New Jersey, recognizing the proposed sculpture to be an integral part of the Hart Building design, established the Capitol Art Foundation for the purpose of raising the $650,000 of private contributions that were required to remunerate the Calder estate and pay for the installation of the sculpture in the atrium.

The Alexander Calder sculpture located in the atrium of the Hart Senate Office Building.

Bust of Senator Carl Trumbull Hayden of Arizona, by the artist Stafford Rolph, now stands on the first floor of the Russell Senate Office Building.

Bust of Senator Henry M. Jackson of Washington, by the artist Ms. Wendy Ross, now stands on the second floor of the Russell Senate Office Building.

Dirksen Senate Office Building.

Hart Senate Office Building.

Capitol Landscape and Improvements

The west front of the Capitol once overlooked marshland, a canal and a railroad station. The Olmsted grounds (1880s) and the design of the Mall (early 20th century) provided the green areas known today.

During the years 1865 through 1900 the Capitol's natural surroundings began to acquire their current grace and dignity. When the Capitol was built the grounds were planted in a rural, informal manner. One writer described the soil at that time as being "exceedingly stiff clay, becoming dust in dry, and mortar in rainy, weather". Only four decades later, however, Mrs. Trollope, the English chronicler, called the grounds an "exceedingly handsome enclosure" and accurately predicted that "in a few years, [they] will offer the shade of all the most splendid trees which flourish in the Union". Today, after several annexations, they comprise a remarkable green oasis in the city. Tourists enjoy them, and Congressional employees relax under the great trees during their lunch hours. The Capitol grounds comprise 212 acres today and contain more than 100 species of plants, shrubs and trees, including the symbolic gifts of State trees from 33 States of the Union. The native species of the Eastern United States predominate, with 13 varieties of maple, 10 varieties of elm and 14 of oak; also planted on the grounds is a giant sequoia, the king of trees, a gift of the State of California.

Not until 1874 were the Capitol grounds embellished by the master landscaper, whose work is abundantly evident today. Frederick Law Olmsted, the greatest landscape architect in

This print from a drawing by Hughson Hawley was done around the turn of the century. It shows the new Olmsted terraces and an Edward Clark proposal for the construction of a pediment and large portico on the west front.

General Plan for the Improvement of the U.S. CAPITOL GROUNDS.

Tulips in bloom on the west front of the Capitol.

Frederick L. Olmsted was hired by the Senate Committee on Buildings and Grounds in 1874 to landscape the Capitol campus. This plan also shows extensions on the Capitol to the west and east.

Tulips among azaleas on the Capitol plaza.

America, came to Washington fresh from his triumph in New York City, where he planned Central Park. Arriving in the Federal City, he remarked that the Capitol grounds were in a state of "sylvan juvenility", and he immediately set to work planning the graceful plantings and walks that have delighted visitors ever since. Mr. Olmsted recognized that the soil of the Capitol grounds was too impoverished to support the extensive plantings he recommended, so his first task was to improve its fertility. His work crews plowed and drained the soil, dressed it with oyster-shell lime and swamp muck, exposed the mix to a winter's frosts, and then topped it all off with a compost of manure and more swamp muck, a necessary process, but one which also must surely have brought a pungent aroma to Capitol Hill during the warm summer months. Olmsted's plans were warmly received by Congress, but on one occasion he found his grand scheme supplanted by the desires of the Senate. One morning in 1875 Senator Simon Cameron of Pennsylvania was

Tulip time at the Capitol.

Crab apple trees on the Senate side.

64

crossing the grounds on his way to the Capitol when he saw a work crew preparing to chop down an ancient and majestic elm near the House which stood in the way of one of Mr. Olmsted's proposed promenades. Senator Cameron demanded that the workmen stop, and then ran to the Senate Chamber where his fellow Members had already begun their session. Begging the floor from the Senator who was speaking at the time, he rose and asked the Senate to express its opinion that the handsome and venerable elm ought to be spared. The tree flourishes today near the House entrance; it has, in fact, been named the "Cameron Elm" in honor of its savior.

Olmsted's work at the Capitol was not confined to landscaping. He was also responsible for the design of a very prominent part of the Capitol's structure: the graceful and dignified west front terraces which replaced Bulfinch's earthen terraces of 1826. He also designed and erected a brick grotto on the Senate side of the grounds with drinking fountains; it has served as a shady retreat for generations of visitors. Yet even as Olmsted proceeded with his work, there were occasional reminders that elegant landscaping and terraces could not change the fact that Washington was still a small city. A routine report filed in 1877, at the height of Mr. Olmsted's activity, recommended that Congress make a special appropriation to replace tender shrubbery and young trees damaged by the cattle that wandered onto the Capitol grounds.

View of the Capitol and the Mall.

Brick grotto with
drinking fountains
located on the Senate
side of the Capitol.

Azaleas in bloom on
the Capitol grounds.

Fountain located in the
park adjacent to the
Russell Senate
Building.

The Capitol from the
Senate side.

Gardens above the House garage.

Cherry Blossom season, east front of the Capitol.

Memorial and Historic Trees

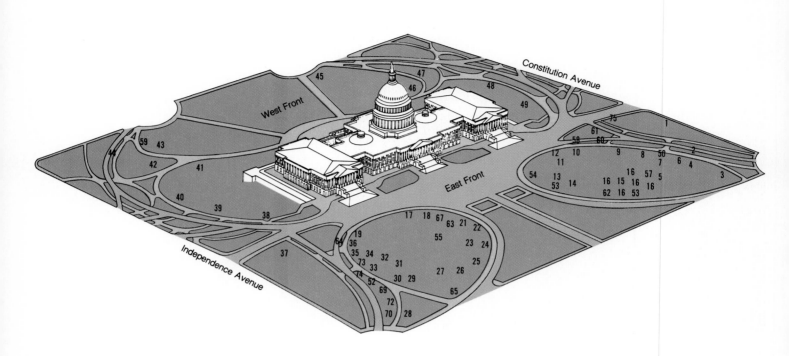

Since the early 1900s, ninety-four memorial and historic trees have been planted. Seventy-three are still living on the Capitol grounds—this chart and guide will help to locate them.

(a) Memorial or historic tree which has been removed from the Capitol grounds.
(b) Memorial tree located in the courtyard of the Russell Building.
(c) Memorial trees located in the lower west court terrace of the Rayburn Building.
(d) Memorial tree located in Square 684, Senate grounds, adjacent to Russell Building.
(e) Memorial tree located at Cannon Building.
(f) Memorial tree located in Square W576, Botanic Garden Conservatory.

Key No.	Date planted	Planted by or memorializing	State	Common name of tree	Botanical name of tree
(a)	Prior to 1800	George Washington	Virginia	American Elm	*Ulmus americana.*
38	Prior to 1875	Senator Simon D. Cameron	Pennsylvania	American Elm	*Ulmus americana.*
(a)	April 18, 1912	Vice President James S. Sherman	New York	Purple Beech	*Fagus sylvatica.*
(a)	April 24, 1912	Senator Augustus O. Bacon	Georgia	Pin Oak	*Quercus palustris.*
44	April 24, 1912	Representative William J. Browning	New Jersey	Red Oak	*Quercus borealis.*
2	April 30, 1912	Senator Jacob H. Gallinger	New Hampshire	Overcup Oak	*Quercus lyrata.*
(a)	May 4, 1912	Senator Henry C. Lodge, Sr.	Massachusetts	Red Oak	*Quercus borealis.*
18	May 4, 1912	Representative James R. Mann	Illinois	Red Oak	*Quercus borealis.*
19	May 7, 1912	Speaker Champ Clark	Missouri	Sugar Maple	*Acer saccharum.*
4	May 9, 1912	Senator Shelby M. Cullom	Illinois	American Elm	*Ulmus americana.*
(a)	May 11, 1912	Senator George P. Wetmore	Rhode Island	American Beech	*Fagus americana.*
(a)	April 21, 1913	Representative Richard Bartholdt (Peace Tree)	Missouri	Pin Oak	*Quercus palustris.*
41	1913	Representative Marlin E. Olmsted	Pennsylvania	Pin Oak	*Quercus palustris.*
34	1913	Speaker Joseph G. Cannon	Illinois	Red Oak	*Quercus borealis.*
33	1916 or 1917	Representative Joseph Taggart	Kansas	Pin Oak	*Quercus palustris.*
(a)	1917 or 1918	Representative Jeannette Rankin	Montana	Redwood	*Sequoia gigantea.*
8	April 8, 1918	Vice President Thomas R. Marshall	Indiana	Hickory	*Hicoria alba.*
13	April 8, 1918	Senator Willard Saulsbury	Delaware	Hickory	*Hicoria alba.*
(a)	1918 or 1919	Representative James L. Slayden	Texas	Pecan	*Hicoria pecan.*
42	1918 or 1919	Representative James L. Slayden	Texas	Pecan	*Hicoria pecan.*
39	1920	Representative Charles H. Randall	California	Redwood	*Sequoia gigantea.*
17	April 15, 1920	Representative Joseph Walsh	Massachusetts	American Beech	*Fagus grandiflora.*
(a)	April 20, 1923	Senator Charles L. McNary	Oregon	Red Oak	*Quercus borealis.*
(a)	May 9, 1925	Mothers' Tree (planted to honor Mothers of America)	All States	White Birch	*Betula laciniata.*
(a)	Nov. 23, 1927	Representative Martin B. Madden	Illinois	Mossycup Oak	*Quercus macrocarpa.*
40	Nov. 26, 1927	Representative David H. Kincheloe	Kentucky	Umbrella Tree	*Magnolia tripetala.*
(a)	May 4, 1928	Representative Roy G. Fitzgerald	Ohio	Bullbay Tree	*Magnolia grandiflora.*
(a)	1929–1933	Vice President Charles Curtis	Kansas	Bullbay Tree	*Magnolia grandiflora.*

Key No.	Date planted	Planted by or memorializing	State	Common name of tree	Botanical name of tree
(a)	May 1929	Senator Simeon D. Fess	Ohio	Buckeye	*Aesculus glabra.*
(a)	April 20, 1931	Boy Scout Tree (from Mount Vernon, VA) first step in nut tree planting program	Virginia	White Walnut	*Juglans cinerea.*
(a)	Dec. 21, 1931	Scion of Washington Elm (from Washington State)	Washington	American Elm	*Ulmus americana.*
(a)	Dec. 21, 1931	Representative Maurice H. Thatcher	Kentucky	American Elm	*Ulmus americana.*
28	April 22, 1932	To honor 100th Anniversary of the Birth of J. Sterling Morton, founder of Arbor Day; and Bicentennial of George Washington	Virginia	Black Walnut	*Juglans nigra.*
30	April 8, 1936	J. Sterling Morton Tree (Representative Karl Stefan, sponsor)	Nebraska	White Pine	*Pinus strobus.*
(a)	Nov. 9, 1939	Sam Houston Centennial Tree (re-planted by Fritz G. Lanham)	Texas	Pecan	*Hicoria pecan.*
15	May 30, 1946	War Memorial Tree (Representative John E. Rankin, sponsor)	All States	White Oak	*Quercus alba.*
6	April 10, 1947	Arbor Day Tree—75th Anniversary of Arbor Day (Senator Kenneth Wherry, sponsor)	Nebraska	Bur Oak	*Quercus macrocarpa.*
27	June 26, 1948	Good Templars Tree (plaque placed on existing tree)		American Elm	*Ulmus americana.*
14	April 16, 1949	Memorial to Senator Thomas P. Gore	Oklahoma	Chestnut Oak	*Quercus prinus.*
49	April 16, 1949	Memorial to Senator Robert L. Owen	Oklahoma	Sweet Gum	*Liquidamber styraciflua.*
35	Oct. 11, 1949	Speaker Sam Rayburn	Texas	White Oak	*Quercus alba.*
32	Sept. 2, 1950	Memorial to Representative Chester C. Bolton	Ohio	Buckeye	*Aesculus glabra.*
11	Nov. 16, 1951	Greater North Dakota Association	North Dakota	American Elm	*Ulmus americana.*
16	June 12, 1952	Memorial to 5 Sullivan Brothers killed in World War II	Iowa	5 Crab Apples	*Pyrus malus.*
5	April 28, 1954	Senator Leverett Saltonstall	Massachusetts	Red Maple	*Acer rubrum.*
25	July 8, 1954	Speaker Joseph W. Martin, Jr.	Massachusetts	English Elm	*Ulmus procera.*
26	May 17, 1955	Michigan State Society	Michigan	White Pine	*Pinus strobus.*
1	Nov. 13, 1963	State of Georgia (Senator Richard B. Russell, sponsor)	Georgia	Loblolly Pine	*Pinus taeda.*
29	Nov. 18, 1963	Representative Carl Vinson	Georgia	White Oak	*Quercus alba.*
21	Nov. 18, 1963	Representative James C. Auchincloss	New Jersey	Red Oak	*Quercus borealis.*
(a)	May 13, 1964	Boys' Clubs of America	All States	Red Pine	*Pinus resinosa.*
36	June 11, 1964	Speaker John W. McCormack	Massachusetts	Sugar Maple	*Acer saccharum.*
23	June 11, 1964	Representative Charles A. Halleck	Indiana	Yellow Poplar	*Liriodendron tulipifera.*
43	March 17, 1965	Potomac Area Council of Camp Fire Girls (commemorating Founders Day)	District of Columbia	Saucer Magnolia	*Magnolia soulangeana.*
3	April 6, 1965	State Society of New Jersey (Senator Clifford P. Case, sponsor)	New Jersey	Northern Red Oak	*Quercus borealis.*
47	May 3, 1965	Senator Jack Miller	Iowa	Black Walnut	*Juglans nigra.*
46	May 20, 1965	Memorial to Senator Robert S. Kerr	Oklahoma	Redbud	*Cercis canadensis.*
(b)	May 26, 1965	State of New Jersey (Senator Harrison A. Williams, Jr., sponsor)	New Jersey	Red Oak	*Quercus borealis.*
(a)	March 29, 1966	Congressional Women's Club (Senators' Wives)		Deodar Cedar	*Cedrus deodara.*
(a)	March 29, 1966	Congressional Women's Club (Representatives' Wives)		Deodar Cedar	*Cedrus deodara.*
48	May 25, 1966	Cherokee Indian Nation (commemorating 200th anniversary of birth of Sequoyah)	Georgia	Redwood	*Sequoia gigantea.*
22	April 3, 1967	State of Ohio (Representative Clarence E. Miller, sponsor)	Ohio	Buckeye	*Aesculus glabra.*
10	April 16, 1967	Arbor Lodge Association of Nebraska City, NE (Senator Carl T. Curtis, sponsor)	Nebraska	Maidenhair	*Ginkgo biloba.*
37	April 28, 1967	Washington Township of New Jersey (Representative John E. Hunt, sponsor)	New Jersey	Cherry Tree	*Prunus Mount Fuji.*
(d)	May 4, 1967	Mrs. Lyndon B. Johnson		Redbud	*Cercis canadensis.*
12	April 30, 1968	Mrs. Lyndon B. Johnson (Senate Wives)		Chinese Dogwood	*Cornus kousa.*
24	May 1, 1969	In Commemoration of the Centennial of Blair, NE (Representative Glenn Cunningham, sponsor)	Nebraska	Blair Maple	*Acer saccarinum Blairi.*
9	June 4, 1969	State of Illinois (dedicated to and planted by Senator Everett M. Dirksen)	Illinois	Pin Oak	*Quercus palustris.*
52	April 14, 1970	State of Tennessee (Representative Richard H. Fulton)	Tennessee	Tulip Poplar	*Liriodendron tulipifera.*
50	Oct. 25, 1971	The Jewish Campaign for the People's Peace Treaty		Bradford Pear	*Pyrus calleryana Bradford.*
51	April 28, 1972	Commemoration of the 100th Anniversary of the First Arbor Day Observance		Japanese Zelkova	*Zelkova serrata.*

Cameron Elm,
circa 1920.

Vice President James
S. Sherman planting a
tree on the Senate
side of the Capitol on
April 18, 1912.

Key No.	Date planted	Planted by or memorializing	State	Common name of tree	Botanical name of tree
54	April 2, 1973	State of Wisconsin (Senator Gaylord Nelson)	Wisconsin	Sugar Maple	*Acer saccharum.*
53	April 10, 1973	The Senate Ladies Gift to Mrs. Richard M. Nixon		Southern Magnolia	*Magnolia grandiflora.*
55	Sept. 26, 1974	In Honor of his Retirement, Representative Dave Martin	Nebraska	American Elm	*Ulmus americana.*
56	Nov. 22, 1974	In Honor of his Retirement, Senator Sam J. Ervin, Jr.	North Carolina	White Dogwood	*Cornus florida.*
57	Dec. 19, 1974	State of Washington (Senator Henry M. Jackson)	Washington	Douglas Fir	*Pseudotsuga taxifolia.*
58	June 10, 1975	Idaho Federation of Women's Clubs (planted by Senator James A. McClure)	Idaho	White Pine	*Pinus strobus.*
(a)	March 12, 1976	In Commemoration of Birthdate of Juliet Gordon Lowe (Girl Scout Council of the National Capital Area)		Sassafras	*Sassafras albidum.*
60	April 5, 1976	State of Maryland (Senator J. Glenn Beall, Jr.)	Maryland	Wye Oak seedling	*Quercus alba var. Wye.*
61	April 27, 1976	In Honor of his Retirement, Senator Roman L. Hruska	Nebraska	Bradford Pear	*Pyrus calleryana Bradford.*
(a)	April 29, 1976	Michigan State Society (Senator Philip A. Hart)	Michigan	American Spruce, Red, White & Blue	*Picea Hybrid.*
63	May 5, 1976	American Mothers Committee, Inc., Honoring Mothers of America		Crape Myrtle	*Lagerstroemia indica.*
64	May 6, 1976	Arbor Day Delegation from Nebraska	Nebraska	Cottonwood	*Populus deltoides.*
(a)	July 7, 1976	Tulare County American Revolution Bi-Centennial Commission (Plano 4-H Bi-Centennial Flag Corp and Porterville High School Choir)	California	Redwood	*Sequoia gigantea.*
66	Nov. 22, 1976	Citizens of Paw Paw, WV	West Virginia	Paw Paw	*Asimina triloba.*
67	Dec. 9, 1976	In Honor of his Retirement, Speaker Carl Albert		Redbud	*Cercis canadensis.*
68	April 29, 1977	National Arbor Day (Representative Hamilton Fish, Senator Jacob K. Javits and Representative Frederick W. Richmond)		Hybrid Elm	*Ulmus Sapporo Autumn Gold.*
(a)	June 6, 1977	1977 Graduation Class (House of Representatives Page School)		Mountain Ash	*Sorbus aucuparia.*
(a)	March 15, 1978	Members of the Texas Delegation, 95th Congress	Texas	Hybrid Pecan	*Carya ill. var. Kiowa.*
71	March 27, 1978	Liberty Tree seedling (Senator Charles McC. Mathias)	Maryland	Tulip Poplar	*Liriodendron tulipifera.*
(c)	May 25, 1978	Republican Congressional Wives Honoring Mrs. Richard Nixon and Mrs. Gerald Ford (Mrs. Gerald Ford)		Golden-chain	*Laburnum anagyroides.*
(a)	June 12, 1978	1978 Graduation Class (House of Representatives Page School)		Mountain Ash	*Sorbus aucuparia.*
(a)	Oct. 5, 1978	California State Society (Representative Fortney H. Stark, Jr.)	California	Redwood	*Sequoia gigantea.*
74	March 23, 1979	In Honor of his Retirement, Representative Olin E. Teague		Bradford Pear	*Pyrus calleryana Bradford.*
75	June 11, 1979	1979 Graduation Class (House of Representatives Page School)		Japanese Pagoda	*Sophora japonica.*
76	April 10, 1980	Honoring First Lady Rosalynn Carter (Senate Wives)		White Dogwood	*Cornus florida.*
77	June 16, 1980	1980 Graduation Class (House of Representatives Page School)		Yoshino Cherry	*Prunus yedoensis.*
78	Nov. 21, 1980	Memorial to Hostages in Iran (Representative Toby Roth)	Wisconsin	Red Oak	*Quercus borealis maxima.*
79	Dec. 4, 1980	In Honor of his Retirement, Representative Harley O. Staggers		Sugar Maple	*Acer saccharum.*
65	Dec. 15, 1980	In Commemoration of the Honorable William M. Colmer		Bullbay Tree	*Magnolia grandiflora.*
80	Dec. 16, 1980	In Honor of his Service in the U.S. Congress, Representative Joseph L. Fisher		White Dogwood	*Cornus florida.*
92	May 26, 1981	South Carolina Forestry Association (Senator Strom Thurmond)	South Carolina	Tulip Poplar	*Liriodendron tulipifera.*
81	June 15, 1981	1981 Graduation Class (Capitol Page School)		Hybrid Blue Spruce	*Picea pungens Hybrid.*
82	July 1, 1981	4-H Club of Nevada County (Representative Gene Chappie)	California	Incensecedar	*Libocedrus decurrens.*
83	Sept. 15, 1981	In Celebration of Pennsylvania's 300th Birthday (Representative Joseph M. Gaydos)	Pennsylvania	Mountain Laurel	*Kalmia latifolia.*
84	Oct. 12, 1981	In Commemoration of the 200th Anniversary of Historic Ride of Jack Jouett (Representative J. Kenneth Robinson)	Virginia	White Dogwood	*Cornus florida.*

Tulip Magnolia and
Cherry Trees on the
Capitol grounds.

U.S. Capitol
Christmas Tree.
Photograph by former
Senator Howard H.
Baker, Jr., of
Tennessee.

Key No.	Date planted	Planted by or memorializing	State	Common name of tree	Botanical name of tree
85	April 29, 1982	Louisiana Statehood Day (Senator Russell B. Long and Senator J. Bennett Johnston)	Louisiana	Bullbay Tree	*Magnolia grandiflora.*
87	May 11, 1982	Honoring the Vietnam Veterans of Minnesota (Representative Arlen Erdahl)	Minnesota	White Oak	*Quercus alba.*
86	May 14, 1982	8th Air Force Historical Society (Representative William S. Broomfield)		Japanese Zelkova	*Zelkova serrata.*
88	June 12, 1982	25th Anniversary of House of Representatives Page School Class of 1957		American Holly	*Ilex opaca.*
89	June 14, 1982	1982 Graduation Class (Capitol Page School)		American Holly	*Ilex opaca.*
90	June 29, 1982	In Honor of Centennial Anniversary of the American Association of University Women (Representative Paul Simon)		White Dogwood	*Cornus florida.*
91	Oct. 30, 1982	Replacement of "Peace Oak" which was removed in 1910		Bur Oak	*Quercus macrocarpa.*
93	March 11, 1983	State of Georgia (Senator Sam Nunn)	Georgia	Dogwood	*Cornus florida.*
(d)	March 21, 1983	State of South Dakota	South Dakota	Black Hills Spruce	*Picea glauca densata.*
94	April 21, 1983	In Honor of his Retirement, Representative William C. Wampler		Sourwood	*Oxydendrum arboreum.*
(e)	April 28, 1983	State of Oregon (Representative Denny Smith)	Oregon	Noble Fir	*Abies procera.*
95	June 20, 1983	1983 Graduation Class (Capitol Page School)		Dogwood	*Cornus florida.*
(e)	Oct. 25, 1983	State of Nevada	Nevada	Jeffrey Pine	*Pinus jeffreyi.*
96	Nov. 15, 1983	In Memory of President John F. Kennedy (Elkins Ward School, Elkins, WV, Senator Jennings Randolph)	West Virginia	Yellow Poplar	*Liriodendron tulipifera.*
97	Jan. 9, 1984	In Honor of Dr. Martin Luther King, Jr.		American Elm	*Ulmus americana,* var. DED Free.
98	March 14, 1984	In Memory of Representative Larry P. McDonald (Representative Charles Hatcher)	Georgia	Dogwood	*Cornus florida.*
(d)	June 8, 1984	U.S. Senate Page School		Bradford Pear	*Pyrus calleryana Bradford.*
(f)	June 14, 1984	U.S. House Page School		Bradford Pear	*Pyrus calleryana Bradford.*
99	Sept. 18, 1984	To Honor Victims of Korean Air Lines Flight 007 (Representative Butler Derrick)	South Carolina	Flowering Peach	*Prunus persica.*
(f)	Sept. 27, 1984	In Honor of his Retirement, Representative Larry Winn, Jr.		Flowering Cherry	*Prunus yedoensis.*
(f)	April 10, 1985	In Memory of Representative Carl D. Perkins	Kentucky	Zelkova	*Zelkova serrata Village Green.*
(b)	April 18, 1985	Mrs. Ronald Reagan (Senate Wives)		Pyramidal English Oak	*Quercus robur fastigiata.*
(f)	April 24, 1985	State of Colorado (Senator William L. Armstrong)	Colorado	Colorado Blue Spruce	*Picea pungens.*
100	April 26, 1985	National Arbor Day (Senator Mark O. Hatfield)		Dawn Redwood	*Metesequoia glyptostroboides.*
(d)	June 3, 1985	U.S. Senate Page School		Sourwood	*Oxydendrum arboreum.*
(e)	June 6, 1985	Oregon Congressional Delegation (Representative Robert F. (Bob) Smith)	Oregon	Western Juniper	*Juniperus var.*
(e)	March 12, 1986	State of Mississippi (Representative Trent Lott)	Mississippi	Bullbay Tree	*Magnolia grandiflora.*
101	May 29, 1986	In honor of Representative Barber B. Conable, Jr.		Tulip Poplar	*Liriodendron tulipifera.*
(d)	June 11, 1986	U.S. Senate Page School		Hybrid English Hawthorn	*Crataegus oxy. Superba.*
(d)	June 11, 1987	U.S. Senate Page School		Katsuratree	*Cercidiphyllum Japonicum.*
(e)	Oct. 8, 1987	Master Gardener Conference (Representative Mike Lowery)	Wisconsin	Douglas Fir	*Pseudotsuga taxifolia.*

Botanic Garden

Summer terrace display.

The U.S. Botanic Garden was founded in 1820 under the auspices of the Columbia Institute for the Promotion of Arts and Sciences, an outgrowth of an association known as the Metropolitan Society, which received its charter from Congress on April 20, 1818. The Botanic Garden continued under the direction of this Institute until 1837, when the Institute ceased to exist as an active organization.

The Botanic Garden thereafter remained abandoned until 1842, when it became necessary for the Government to provide accommodations for the botanical collections brought to Washington, D.C. from the South Seas by the U.S. Exploring Expedition of 1838–42, under the leadership of Captain Charles Wilkes. The collection was temporarily placed on exhibition on a lot behind the Patent Office Building. A greenhouse was constructed under the direction and control of the Joint Committee on the Library.

Upon completion of the greenhouse the collection from the exploring expedition was placed therein and was put under the custodianship of the Commissioner of Patents by the Library Committee. The actual care of the botanical collections was under the supervision of Captain Wilkes, assisted by William D. Brackenridge, a horticulturist and assistant botanist for the expedition.

In 1849 Congress authorized the construction of an extension to the Patent Office Building making it necessary to relocate the Botanic Garden greenhouses to the west end of the Capitol grounds, practically the same location as that occupied by the Botanic Garden during the period it functioned under the Columbia Institute. The construction of a new greenhouse on this site was placed under the supervision of the Architect of the Capitol, with the approval of the Joint Committee on the Library.

U.S. Botanic Garden.

For many years following this relocation, the Congress was interested in securing for the Botanic Garden more adequate facilities for carrying on its work, to place it on a level with other botanic gardens throughout the country.

On January 7, 1925, Congress took definite steps toward this goal by authorizing the preparation of preliminary plans for the construction of new conservatories and other necessary buildings and for the relocation of the Bartholdi Fountain.

The Bartholdi Fountain was originally exhibited at the 1876 International Exhibition held in Philadelphia, and had been purchased by the U.S. Government in 1877 for $6,000. The architect of the fountain was Frederic Auguste Bartholdi, a French sculptor who also designed the Statue of Liberty. The fountain, cast in Paris by A. Dureene, is constructed of cast iron painted to look like bronze. The entire structure is 30 feet high and is designed symmetrically in three identical sections. The triangulated base with turtle-like aquatic monsters and large shells rises to the pedestal holding three identical female nereids (sea nymphs). The curved arms of the nymphs seem to hold up the large basin, actually supported by the central column. This basin supports twelve lights which were originally gas lamps. The fountain is surmounted by a mural crown resembling a crenelated city wall through which the water flows.

Spring flower show.

Interior of the Conservatory.

Bartholdi Fountain.

The cornerstone of the new conservatory was laid on November 12, 1931; the new buildings were occupied on January 13, 1933.

Structurally, the design of the new conservatory follows conventional form, with an arched and domed roof frame carrying the great expanse of glass sheathing. In its details the design presents many points of interest, among which is the extensive use of aluminum for structural members—the first time aluminum had been used for such purposes. The main feature is the one-story loggia or entrance hall forming the Maryland Avenue front. It is built of limestone, carried to a height of about 40 feet and has a series of lofty arched doorways. The main conservatory is 262 feet in length and 183 feet in width.

The square across Independence Avenue, south of the Conservatory, was developed as an outdoor garden—this is the site of the relocated Bartholdi Fountain. In 1986 the park was named the Frederick Auguste Bartholdi Park in honor of the sculptor as part of the year long observation of the 100th anniversary of the Statue of Liberty.

The Botanic Garden property also includes more than 22 acres known as Poplar Point Nursery, adjacent to Anacostia Park. This property was added to the U.S. Botanic Garden in 1926.

Chrysanthemum show.

Interior orchid collection.

Desert plants.

74

Interior courtyard of Botanic Garden in the springtime.

The Frederick Auguste Bartholdi Park.

Music at the Capitol

Music, Maestro

The Capitol and the House and Senate office buildings resound, especially during the spring and summer months, with all types of music. From the majestic inspiration of the National Symphony, and the stirring marches of the military bands to the tunes of Gershwin and the tones of Roberta Flack, the visitors to the Capitol can enjoy whatever suits their taste.

The American Festival/Concerts at the Capitol are sponsored by the United States Congress and the Secretary of the Interior. They are performed by the National Symphony and have been conducted by such maestros as Aaron Copland, Leonard Bernstein, Mstislav Rostropovich and Erich Leinsdorf. These performances have delighted hundreds of thousands of music lovers from all over the world.

The Service bands, and choral groups, of the Air Force, Army, Marine Corps and Navy provide summer night entertainment for other thousands in concerts that have become a Capitol tradition.

Perhaps more thrilling to the individual musicians concerned are the hundreds of performances every spring by the high school and college bands from all over the United States which perform on the Capitol steps. In addition the Capitol and its various office buildings are filled throughout the year, but especially during the winter holiday season, with the joyous voices of choral groups.

These appearances are arranged well in advance by the Senators or Representatives through the Architect of the Capitol.

Without this music the Capitol would be a far more somber place indeed.

A member of the Air Force Band performs at the Capitol. Note the reflection of the Capitol in the instrument.

The President's Own, the Marine Band performing on the west front of the Capitol.

The Lake Shore Shorian Marching Band from Michigan on the steps of the west front of the Capitol.

The National Symphony performs on the west lawn of the Capitol.

77

A high school group entertains on the House steps.

The Army Band performs at the Capitol.

The Air Force Band performs as hundreds listen on the steps of the west front of the Capitol.

The Sea Chanters of the Navy Band perform the Man from La Mancha at the Capitol.

The Navy Band performs at the Capitol.

A visiting choral group performs in the Russell Senate Office Building rotunda.

The Marine Band at the Capitol.

A noontime performance at the Library of Congress.

A high school band from Sacramento, California, performs at the Capitol.

The Army Band at the Capitol.

The Las Estralles del Sol's participating in the American Folklife Series at the Capitol.

79

Congress as an Institution

Copyright © Fred J. Maroon

1 Capitol
2 House
3 Senate
4 Russell Senate Office Building
5 Dirksen Senate Office Building
6 Hart Senate Office Building
7 Adams Building, Library of Congress
8 Jefferson Building, Library of Congress
9 Madison Building, Library of Congress
10 Cannon House Office Building
11 House Annex No. 1
12 Longworth House Office Building
13 Rayburn House Office Building
14 Botanic Garden
15 House Annex No. 2

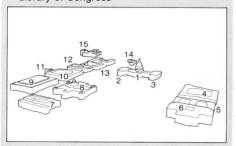

Courtesy of the Architect of the Capitol's Office-1988

The United States House of Representatives

*Official portrait
of the United States
House of Representatives,
April 3, 1987*

Courtesy of the United States Capitol Historical Society.

The Congress was created by Article I of the Constitution which vests all legislative powers granted by the people to the Government in the Senate and the House of Representatives. Section 1 of Article I establishes the specific structure and powers of the House of Representatives.

Currently the House is limited to 435 Representatives elected by the voters of the 50 states. In addition, one Delegate each represents the voters of American Samoa, the District of Columbia, Guam, and the Virgin Islands. Puerto Rico is represented by a Resident Commissioner. These latter five persons do not vote on the passage of bills, although they do vote in committee to approve a bill to be considered by the total House.

States are assigned the number of Representatives based on the decennial census. Each Member represents approximately 517,000 constituents. Each state is entitled to at least one Representative, even though the population of the state may be less than 517,000. The state legislature defines the geographic boundaries of the Congressional district whose voters elect a Representative every 2 years. If a Representative dies or leaves office in midterm the Governor of the state calls a special election to choose a replacement.

Any citizen over the age of 25, who has been a citizen of the United States for at least 7 years, may be elected to serve in the House of Representatives, providing that he or she is a resident of the state at the time of election. Senators must be 30 years of age and a resident of their state.

Unlike the Senate, whose Members represent the states, the Representatives' powers do not overlap those of the executive and judicial branches of the Federal Government. They do not confirm Presidential appointments. The House does not vote on ratification of treaties. The House can vote on articles of impeachment, i.e., an indictment of the President or other Federal officer, but the Senate judges whether or not the officer is removed from office.

The major strength of the House lies in its power to initiate "money" bills—taxation and appropriation measures. The Senate may vote changes in such bills, but the differences are resolved in conference between the House and Senate.

Because of the large number of Representatives, the House has of necessity developed more restrictive rules on debate than those which apply to the Senate. The Rules Committee of the House determines the order in which bills come to the floor for action, the time limit during which a bill may be considered, whether or not—and how many—amendments to the bill may be proposed.

As in the Senate, the major activity of the House, especially in the early months of each session, is in the committees, which receive all bills introduced on the subject of a committee's jurisdiction. The committees are divided into subcommittees which conduct hearings, add amendments and either approve or reject the bills. If approved, the bill is considered by the full committee which can reject, amend and approve, or decline to act on the measure. If approved, the bill goes to the Rules Committee for scheduling for floor action.

When a bill is granted a rule, it comes before the House which resolves itself into the Committee of the Whole. In this status the House debates the bill, considers and accepts or rejects amendments. The Committee of the Whole then resolves itself into the House of Representatives and votes on each amendment and lastly on final passage.

The House meets in the House Chamber in the south wing of the Capitol. Members are not assigned specific seats as in the Senate. The majority party members sit on the right of the Speaker's rostrum, the minority on the left. As in the Senate Chamber, the press and media galleries are above the Speaker's rostrum. The public is seated in the side and rear galleries; seats are available to those who secure passes from their Representatives on a first come, first served basis.

The Mace of the House of Representatives, topped by a flying eagle, is the ensign of authority. Its significance is not merely symbolic since the position of the Mace is a signal to the Members of the activity taking place in the Chamber. An Assistant Sergeant at Arms sets it at the right of the Speaker when the House is called to order each day. There it remains in position while the House is in session. Its removal to a lower pedestal means the House has resolved itself into a Committee of the Whole House on the State of the Union. Thus Members can see whether the House is in session or in committee. These signals are important because 218 Members constitute a quorum for action in the House and only 100 when the House is assembled in the Committee of the Whole. William Adams of New York reproduced this 46-inch Mace in 1841 from the design of its predecessor which the British destroyed by fire in 1814. It is a superb example of the silversmith's art, but cost the United States only $400. Today it is worth much more and historically and sentimentally it is beyond value.

Jack Russ, Sergeant at Arms of the House, holds the Mace, which is the symbol of legislative power and authority in the House of Representatives.

Chamber of the House of Representatives

The President of the United States most often addresses the Congress in the Chamber of the House of Representatives in a joint session. The counting of electoral ballots for the Presidency is done in a joint session every four years. Any other occasion wherein notables address the Congress is referred to as a joint meeting.

The Speaker of the House and the President of the Senate sit on the top dais in this set of three. The President, ministers, kings, diplomats, heads of state and public personalities of the first magnitude, in addressing a joint gathering of Members of the House and Senate in this Chamber, speak from the intermediary dais.

The U.S. flag is centered behind the Speaker's desk, flanked on either side by the fasces—rods and ax—symbols of the authority of the ancient Roman magistrates. The doors on each side of the dais lead to the Speaker's lobby. Full length portraits of Washington and Lafayette hang to the left and the right of the doors.

Above the clock is the gallery for the press. In the other galleries the heavy television, newsreel and photographic equipment of the communications industry is located. This Chamber has three times the floor area of the British House of Commons and is the largest national parliamentary room in the world. Here for the verdict of Congress were heard the Presidential messages that took the country into war, mobilizing 4,355,000 men in World War I and more than 16 million in World War II.

The flag behind the Speaker, the brass fasces on either side of the flag, the American eagle surrounded by 50 stars in the center of the ceiling, and the colorful seals of each state forming the border decoration of the ceiling are symbols of our freedom in this historic Chamber that the House has occupied since 1857.

In 1973 an electronic voting system was installed to expedite the voting process. Components of this system are located on the walls behind and above the Speaker.

Located below the galleries on each side of the House Chamber, summary display panels present running tabulations as well as the time remaining for the vote in progress.

An individual Representative's vote is displayed on panels above the Speaker's chair while a vote is in progress in the House Chamber.

The Speaker

Foremost Man of His Party in the House, The Speaker is Third in Line and Second in Succession to the Presidency.

The Speaker of the House is one of the most powerful office holders in the U.S. Government, surpassed only by the President and Vice President. The Presidential Succession Act of 1947 places the Speaker second in line in succession to the Presidency, behind only the Vice President, whose assumption to that office is required by the Constitution.

Selecting a Speaker

In the early days the Speaker was elected by ballot, but since 1859 all have been chosen by roll call or voice vote. The election of the Speaker is traditionally the first order of business of the House upon the convening of a new Congress.

The choosing of the Speaker has undergone a few significant changes over the past 190 years. Only relatively senior members with 20-plus years

of experience have been elected Speaker in this century. From 1789 to 1896, each new Speaker averaged only seven years of experience in Congress. Once elected, a Speaker is customarily re-elected as long as his party remains in the majority and he retains his Congressional seat.

Although the election officially occurs on the floor of the House, modern-day Speakers are actually decided upon when the majority party meets in caucus on the eve of a new Congress. Despite the foregone conclusion of the contest, the minority party also nominates its candidate who, upon losing, becomes minority leader. Since the 1930s, service in the lesser party-leadership posts, such as majority and minority whip, majority and minority leader, have become stepping stones to the Speakership.

The stability of the two-party system in the modern era has led to a period of unbroken lines of succession in the leadership ranks of both parties. This has not always been the case, however. In 1855, more than 130 separate votes were required over a period of two months before a Speaker was finally chosen. In 1859, only four years later, the House balloted 44 times before choosing a first-term New Jersey Congressman for the Speakership—and he was defeated for re-election to the House after that one term.

Powers and Duties

The Constitution makes a scant reference to the office, prescribing in Article I, Section 2 that "the House of Representatives shall chuse [sic] their speaker." While the powers and duties of the Speaker are spelled out to some degree in the *Rules of the House*, the effectiveness of any particular Speaker has depended upon a great many intangibles: the Speaker's own personality, the size of his majority in the House, his relationship with the executive branch, his ability to "get things done." Men of greatly differing styles and temperaments have served as Speaker. Freshmen, septuagenarians,

President Reagan, Speaker Jim Wright and House Republican Leader Robert H. Michel.

dictators, tyrants, moderates, Southerners, Northerners, one future President, two future Vice Presidents (and would-be Presidents) have all, at one time or another, served as the Speaker.

In the modern era, the many duties of the Speaker include presiding at the sessions of the House, announcing the order of business, putting questions to a vote, reporting the vote and deciding points of order. He appoints the chairmen of the Committee of the Whole and members of select and conference committees. He chooses Speakers pro tempore and refers bills and reports to the appropriate committees and calendars. Although he is not constitutionally required to be an elected Member of the House, this *de facto* requirement assures that the Speaker also enjoys the privilege of ordinary House Members. He may, therefore, after stepping down from the Chair, vote and participate in debate on the floor.

Perhaps the duties of the Speaker were put most idealistically by the first "great" Speaker, Henry Clay, in 1823. It was up to the Speaker to be prompt and impartial in deciding questions of order, to display "patience, good temper and courtesy" to every Member and to make "the best arrangement and distribution of the talent of the House" in carrying out the country's business. Finally, Clay noted, the Speaker must "remain cool and unshaken amidst all the storms of debate, carefully guarding the preservation of the permanent laws and rules of the House from being sacrificed to temporary passions, prejudices or interests." But in fact the Speakership today is a partisan office. As Floyd Riddick, Parliamentarian Emeritus of the U.S. Senate, has commented, "tradition and unwritten law require that the Speaker apply the rules of the House consistently, yet in the twilight zone a large area exists where he may exercise great discrimination and where he has many opportunities to apply the rules to his party's advantage."

Triple Personality

The Speaker of the House has three jobs—he is a Member of the House, its presiding officer and leader of the majority party in the Chamber. As a Member of the House he has the right to cast his vote on all questions, unlike the President of the Senate (the Vice President) who has no vote

except in the case of a tie. Usually, however, the Speaker does not exercise his right to vote except to break a tie or when he desires to make his position known on a measure before the House. As a Member he also has the right to leave the Chair and participate in debate on the House floor as the elected Representative of his district.

As presiding officer of the House the Speaker interprets the rules that the House has adopted for guidance. In this matter he is customarily bound by precedents, created by prior decision of the Chair. Appeals are usually in order from decisions of the Chair, but seldom occur. When they are taken, the Chair is usually sustained. The Speaker's power of recognition is partially limited by House rules and conventions that fix the time for considerations of various classes of bills.

He has discretion in recognizing the Members moving to suspend the rules. The rules of the House may be suspended by two-thirds vote on the

first and third Mondays of the month, the Tuesdays immediately following those days and the final six days of the session.

As a party leader, the Speaker had certain additional powers prior to 1910: to appoint all standing committees and to name their chairmen; to select members of the Rules Committee; and to serve as its chairman. His political power evolved gradually during the nineteenth century and peaked under the leadership of former Speaker Joseph Cannon.

In 1910, the House cut back some of the Speaker's power. They removed him from the Rules Committee, stripped him of his power to appoint the standing House committees and their chairmen and restricted his right of recognition. These actions were not directed so much against the principle of leadership as against the concentration of power in the hands of a single individual.

The Speaker with his wife, Betty, and Lady Bird Johnson.

The Speaker and Representative Jack Brooks of Texas.

Biography in Brief of the Speaker

The Speaker issues the oath of office to the Members of the House of Representatives.

Jim Wright of Fort Worth, Texas was elected 48th Speaker of the U.S. House of Representatives on January 6, 1987. Appropriately, that date also marked the 105th anniversary of the birth of another great Texan, Sam Rayburn, who served as Speaker longer than anyone else in American history.

Speaker Wright was born in Fort Worth, Texas on December 22, 1922, the son of James C. Wright and Marie Lyster Wright. He completed public school in 10 years and was on his way toward finishing college in three years when Pearl Harbor was attacked. Enlisting in the Army Air Corps, Mr. Wright received his flyer's wings and a commission. He flew combat missions in the South Pacific and holds the Distinguished Flying Cross and the Legion of Merit.

After the war, Mr. Wright was elected to the Texas Legislature at 23. At 26, he became the youngest Mayor in Texas when voters chose him to head the city government in Weatherford, his boyhood home. In 1953, he served as President of the Texas League of Municipalities.

In 1954, he was elected to the U.S. House of Representatives and has been reelected to each succeeding Congress. He is currently serving his 17th term as Representative from Texas' 12th District.

In 1976, his Democratic colleagues elected him to be Majority Leader, and he was reelected in each of the next four Congresses. In 1987, the historic 100th Congress elected him to be Speaker.

The Speaker meets with the President at the White House.

Speaker Wright at home in Texas.

Mr. Wright is the author of major legislation in the fields of foreign affairs, economic development, water conservation, education and energy. A prolific writer, he has authored four widely acclaimed books: *The Coming Water Famine, You and Your Congressman, Of Swords and Plowshares,* and *Reflections of a Public Man.*

On weekends, when he is not making speeches for his colleagues back in their districts, Mr. Wright likes to work in his garden in McLean, Virginia.

He is married to the former Betty Hay and has four children.

The Speaker and his wife, Betty.

Speaker Wright leads Democratic combo— House Chaplain James D. Ford, former Representative William Boner of Tennessee, Representatives J.J. Pickle of Texas and David Obey of Wisconsin.

The Speaker is an avid sportsman.

Former Speakers

Since Frederick A. C. Muhlenberg was elected in 1789, there have been 47 Speakers, from 20 different States. One, James K. Polk of Tennessee, served as President of the United States. Two, Schuyler Colfax of Indiana and John Nance Gardner of Texas, later served as Vice President.

Sam Rayburn of Texas served as Speaker the longest: over 17 years; Thomas P. O'Neill, Jr. of Massachusetts had the longest continuous service: ten years. Theodore M. Pomeroy of New York served the shortest term: one day.

Frederick A. C. Muhlenberg, Pennsylvania: The first Speaker of the House of Representatives. Served during both the First and Third Congresses, April 1, 1789 to March 3, 1791, and December 2, 1793 to March 3, 1795.

Jonathan Trumbull, Connecticut: Second to occupy the Speakership of the House. Presided over Second Congress from October 24, 1791 to March 2, 1793.

Jonathan Dayton, New Jersey: Speaker, Fourth, and first session of Fifth Congresses, December 7, 1795 to March 3, 1797, and May 15, 1797 to July 10, 1797.

Theodore Sedgwick, Massachusetts: Speaker, Sixth Congress, December 2, 1799 to March 3, 1801.

Nathaniel Macon, North Carolina: Speaker, Seventh, Eighth, and Ninth Congresses, December 7, 1801 to March 3, 1807.

Joseph B. Varnum,
Massachusetts: Speaker for Tenth and
Eventh Congresses, October 26, 1807 to
March 3, 1811.

Henry Clay,
Kentucky: Speaker Twelfth and Thirteenth
(resigned), Fourteenth, Fifteenth, first
session of the Sixteenth, and Eighteenth
Congresses, November 4, 1811 to January
19, 1814, December 4, 1815 to October 28,
1820, December 1, 1823 to March 3, 1825.

Landon Cheves,
South Carolina: Elected Speaker during
second session of Thirteenth Congress,
January 19, 1814 to March 3, 1815.

John W. Taylor,
New York: Speaker, second session
Sixteenth Congress, and Nineteenth
Congress, November 15, 1820 to March 3,
1821, and December 5, 1825 to March 3,
1827.

Philip P. Barbour,
Virginia: Speaker Seventeenth Congress,
December 4, 1821 to March 3, 1823.

Andrew Stevenson,
Virginia: Speaker, Twentieth, Twenty-first,
Twenty-second, and first session Twenty-
third Congresses from December 3, 1827 to
June 2, 1834.

John Bell,
Tennessee: Speaker, first session Twenty-third Congress, from June 2, 1834 to March 3, 1835.

James K. Polk,
Tennessee: Speaker, Twenty-fourth and Twenty-fifth Congresses from December 7, 1835 to March 3, 1839. Eleventh President of the United States.

Robert M. T. Hunter,
Virginia: Speaker, Twenty-sixth Congress, December 16, 1839 to March 3, 1841.

John White,
Kentucky: Speaker of the Twenty-seventh Congress, May 31, 1841 to March 3, 1843.

John W. Jones,
Virginia: Speaker, Twenty-eighth Congress, December 4, 1843 to March 3, 1845.

John Wesley Davis,
Indiana: Speaker, Twenty-ninth Congress, December 1, 1845 to March 3, 1847.

Robert C. Winthrop,
Massachusetts: Speaker, Thirtieth
Congress, December 6, 1847 to March 3,
1849.

Howell Cobb,
Georgia: Speaker, Thirty-first Congress,
December 22, 1849 to March 3, 1851.

Linn Boyd,
Kentucky: Speaker, Thirty-second, Thirty-
third Congresses, December 1, 1851 to
March 3, 1855.

Nathaniel P. Banks,
Massachusetts: Speaker, Thirty-fourth
Congress, February 2, 1856 to March 3,
1857.

James L. Orr,
South Carolina: Speaker, Thirty-fifth
Congress, December 7, 1857 to March 3,
1859.

William Pennington,
New Jersey: Speaker, Thirty-sixth
Congress, February 1, 1860 to March 3,
1861.

Galusha A. Grow,
Pennsylvania: Speaker, Thirty-seventh
Congress, July 4, 1861 to March 3, 1863.

Schuyler Colfax,
Indiana: Speaker, Thirty-eighth through the
Fortieth Congresses, from December 7,
1863 to March 3, 1869. Later served as Vice
President.

Theodore M. Pomeroy,
New York: Speaker last day of Fortieth
Congress, March 3, 1869.

James G. Blaine,
Maine: Speaker of the Forty-first through
the Forty-third Congresses, from March 4,
1869 to March 3, 1875.

Michael C. Kerr,
Indiana: Speaker, Forty-fourth Congress,
first session, December 6, 1875 to
August 19, 1876.

Samuel J. Randall,
Pennsylvania: Speaker, second session of
Forty-fourth through the Forty-sixth
Congresses, from December 4, 1876 to
March 3, 1881.

J. Warren Keifer,
Ohio: Speaker, Forty-seventh Congress, December 5, 1881 to March 3, 1883.

John G. Carlisle,
Kentucky: Speaker, Forty-eighth through the Fiftieth Congresses, December 3, 1883 to March 3, 1889.

Thomas B. Reed,
Maine: Speaker, Fifty-first, Fifty-fourth, Fifty-fifth Congresses, December 2, 1889 to March 2, 1891, and from December 2, 1895 to March 3, 1899.

Charles F. Crisp,
Georgia: Speaker, Fifty-second and Fifty-third Congresses from December 8, 1891 to March 3, 1895.

David B. Henderson,
Iowa: Speaker, Fifty-sixth and Fifty-seventh Congresses, from December 4, 1899 to March 3, 1903.

Joseph G. Cannon,
Illinois: Speaker, Fifty-eighth through Sixty-first Congresses, from November 9, 1903 to March 3, 1911.

James Beauchamp Clark,
Missouri: Speaker, Sixty-second through
Sixty-fifth Congresses, from April 4, 1911
to March 3, 1919.

Frederick H. Gillett,
Massachusetts: Speaker, Sixty-sixth
through Sixty-eighth Congresses, from
May 19, 1919 to March 3, 1925.

Nicholas Longworth,
Ohio: Speaker, Sixty-ninth through
Seventy-first Congresses, from December 7,
1925 to March 3, 1931.

John Nance Garner,
Texas: Speaker, Seventy-second Congress,
from December 7, 1931 to March 3, 1933.
Later served as Vice President.

Henry T. Rainey,
Illinois: Speaker, Seventy-third Congress,
from March 9, 1933 to June 18, 1934.

Joseph W. Byrns,
Tennessee: Speaker, Seventy-fourth
Congress, from January 3, 1935 to June 4,
1936.

William B. Bankhead,
Alabama: Elected Speaker, during the Seventy-fourth Congress, served until death in Seventy-sixth Congress, June 4, 1936 to September 15, 1940.

Sam Rayburn,
Texas: Elected Speaker during the 76th Congress, served through the 79th Congress, then the 81st and 82nd Congresses, and 84th–87th Congresses (died after first session) from September 16, 1940 to August 2, 1946, January 3, 1949 to July 7, 1952, and January 5, 1955 to November 16, 1961.

Joseph W. Martin, Jr.,
Massachusetts: Speaker, Eightieth Congress and Eighty-third Congress, from January 3, 1947 to December 31, 1948, and January 3, 1953 to August 20, 1954.

John W. McCormack,
Massachusetts: Speaker, second session, Eighty-seventh Congress through Ninety-first Congress, from January 10, 1962 to January 2, 1971.

Carl Albert,
Oklahoma: Speaker, Ninety-second through Ninety-fourth Congresses, from January 21, 1971 to January 3, 1977.

Thomas P. O'Neill, Jr.,
Massachusetts: Speaker, Ninety-fifth through Ninety-ninth Congresses, from January 3, 1977 to January 6, 1987.

The House Majority Leader

Majority Leader Tom Foley often serves as spokesman for the House leadership.

National security issues are a major focus for the Majority Leader as a member of the Permanent Select Committee on Intelligence.

Representative Thomas S. Foley of Washington was unanimously elected majority leader in 1987 at the start of the 100th Congress. He is the 16th majority leader since 1911, when Oscar Underwood of Alabama became the first person elected to the job, and he is the first Member from west of the Rocky Mountains to serve in the post.

Tom Foley was born in Spokane, Washington, a city he now represents in Congress as part of the State's 5th Congressional district. A graduate of the University of Washington and its School of Law, he served as an assistant attorney general for the State of Washington and as deputy prosecutor for Spokane County. Before his election to Congress in 1964, he also served on the Senate Interior Commit-

tee staff as a Special Counsel to the late Senator Henry M. Jackson.

During his years in Congress Representative Foley has been a member of the Interior Committee and the Agriculture Committee, of which he was Chairman from 1975 through 1980. He is also a former Chairman of the House Democratic Caucus and the Democratic Study Group. For the six years prior to his election as Majority Leader, he served as Majority Whip, the third highest position in the House Democratic leadership. In addition to his current duties as Majority Leader, he also serves on the Budget Committee and the Permanent Select Committee on Intelligence. He is also Chairman of the Geneva Arms Talks Observer Team.

Representative Foley's careful, even-handed manner and low-key demeanor serve him well as Majority Leader. He is widely esteemed as a coalition builder among the different groups in the House. He has won praise for his parliamentary expertise, his grasp of complex issues, his legislative skill and his ability to forge a consensus.

Representative Foley deals with a wide range of defense questions as Chairman of the Geneva Arms Talks Observer Team.

The Majority Leader is proud of his eastern Washington heritage—agriculture, trade, natural resources and the environment are several of the area's major concerns.

The House Republican Leader

Representative Bob Michel was elected House Republican Leader of the 97th Congress on December 8, 1980. Prior to that, he served in two other House Republican leadership offices. He was Republican Whip during the 94th, 95th, and 96th Congresses spanning the years 1975–1980. He served as Chairman of the National Republican Campaign Committee during the 93rd Congress from 1973–1974.

Robert Henry Michel was born in Peoria, Illinois on March 2, 1923. He was reared and educated in Peoria and was graduated from Bradley University with a B.S. degree in Business Administration in 1948. Michel received the Bradley University Distinguished Alumni Award in 1961, and he holds honorary doctorate degrees from Illinois Wesleyan University, Lincoln College, Illinois College, Bradley University and Bellarmine College.

During World War II, Michel served in the enlisted ranks as a combat infantryman in England, France, Belgium and Germany. He was wounded by machine gun fire in the Battle of the Bulge and discharged as a disabled veteran after being awarded two Bronze Stars, the Purple Heart and four battle stars.

Michel first came to Washington as the administrative assistant to his predecessor, Representative Harold Velde in 1949 and served in that position until 1956. He was elected to the 85th Congress upon Velde's retirement and has been re-elected to 15 consecutive terms since then. He served for a short period on the Committee on Government Operations and in 1958 became a member of the House Appropriations Committee. The Illinois Representative served on the Appropriations Subcommittee on Agriculture and as ranking Republican on the Labor, Health, Education and Welfare Appropriations Subcommittee and the Legislative Appropriations Subcommittee.

Long active in Republican politics, Michel has been a delegate to every Republican National Convention since 1964 and was chairman of the Platform Subcommittee on Human Resources in 1972 and 1980. Michel was Deputy Floor Leader for President Gerald R. Ford in 1976, and Floor Leader for President Reagan in 1980.

During those rare moments when he is not engaged in Congressional or leadership duties, Representative Michel is usually found enjoying his two favorite pastimes: singing, in a rich bass voice that has become familiar at gatherings on Capitol Hill, and playing golf. For many years he was the pitcher for the Republican baseball team in its annual duel with Congressional Democrats, winning fifteen out of seventeen starting assignments.

Bob Michel is married to the former Corinne Woodruff of Peoria. The couple has four children, three sons, Scott, Bruce, and Robin, and a daughter, Laurie. The Michels also have three grandchildren.

House Republican Leader Bob Michel of Illinois in his Capitol Office.

House Republican Leader Michel with a fellow member of the House Republican Leadership, Representative Dick Cheney.

An accomplished singer, Representative Michel opened the Republican National Convention in 1980 by singing the National Anthem.

Representative Michel has participated in a number of golf tournaments for charity over the years.

House Leadership

At the beginning of each Congress, the leadership of the House of Representatives is elected. The Constitution authorizes the House to elect a Speaker. Each party caucus also elects its party leader. Under the tradition of the two party system in this country, the leader of the party with the largest number of Members becomes the Majority Leader. The Minority Leader is invariably the Member nominated by the minority party for the Speaker.

The Majority Leader works very closely with the Speaker in developing the party's position on major policy issues. He almost always has represented a different geographic area of the country from the Speaker. He consults with committee chairmen and urges them to move legislation which the party considers important.

House Democratic leadership: (left to right) Tony Coelho of California, Whip; Tom Foley of Washington, Majority Leader; Jim Wright of Texas, Speaker; Richard Gephardt of Missouri, Caucus Chairman; David Bonior of Michigan, Chief Deputy Whip.

Chairman of the Democratic Congressional Campaign Committee, Beryl Anthony of Arkansas.

In his Capitol office, Speaker Jim Wright of Texas, discusses the day's schedule with his senior staff, Kathy Mitchell, executive assistant, Marshall Lynam, chief of staff, and John Mack, staff director of the Democratic Steering and Policy Committee.

Each party also appoints a whip and assistant whips to assist the floor leader in execution of the party's legislative program. The main job of the whips is to canvass party members on a pending issue and give the floor leader an accurate estimate of the support or opposition expected on a bill. The term "whip" refers to the responsibility of these Members to pressure the other Members of their party to the floor for key votes.

In recent years the majority party has revitalized the Caucus of its Members and the Chairman of the Caucus, elected by his party colleagues, has become an important part of the leadership structure.

House Republican Leader Robert H. Michel of Illinois, (center) in his Capitol office (H–232) with Floor Assistant Bill Pitts (left) and Administrative Assistant Sharon Yard (right).

House Republican leadership for the 100th Congress: (front row) Policy Committee Chairman Jerry Lewis of California; Republican Whip Trent Lott of Mississippi; Republican Leader Robert H. Michel of Illinois; Conference Chairman Dick Cheney of Wyoming; Research Committee Chairman Mickey Edwards of Oklahoma. (back row) Ranking Members, Ways and Means Committee John J. Duncan of Tennessee; Ranking Member on the Budget Committee Delbert L. Latta of Ohio; Ranking Member of the Rules Committee James H. Quillen of Tennessee; Conference Vice-Chairman Lynn Martin of Illinois; Conference Secretary Robert J. Lagomarsino of California; National Republican Congressional Committee Chairman Guy Vander Jagt of Michigan; Ranking Member on the Appropriations Committee Silvio O. Conte of Massachusetts.

101

Elected Officers of the House

At the beginning of each session of Congress both bodies, by majority vote, elect the officers whose responsibility it is to keep the House and Senate operating smoothly. These persons are not Members of the Congress. The House elects the Clerk of the House, the Sergeant at Arms of the House, the Postmaster of the House, and the Chaplain of the House.

Clerk of the House

This office has a broad range of legislative and administrative duties. These include presiding at the opening of each new Congress, pending the election of the Speaker; receiving the credentials of Members; compiling the Official Role of Representatives-elect; taking all votes and certifying passage of bills; processing all legislation, maintaining, printing and distributing documents relating to the legislative activity. The Clerk also receives all official communications during recess or adjournment periods.

A number of internal budgeting, disbursing, accounting and housekeeping responsibilities are also assigned to the Clerk. This officer is assisted by the Offices of Finance, Supply Service, Equipment Service and Records and Registration. There are 18 various departments that operate under the direction of the Clerk to administer these functions.

Donnald K. Anderson, Clerk of the House.

Sergeant at Arms of the House

This office enforces the rules of the House and maintains decorum during sessions of the House. The Sergeant at Arms also is in charge of the Mace, the symbol of legislative power and authority.

Maintaining the general security of the House buildings and the Capitol is his major responsibility.

This officer alternates with the Senate Sergeant at Arms as Chairman of the Capitol Police Board and the Capitol Guide Board. Another major responsibility is management of the House bank which disburses Members' salaries and travel expenses.

Jack Russ, Sergeant at Arms.

Jack Russ, Sergeant at Arms, with Laura Newman, his Executive Assistant.

Doorkeeper of the House

Physical arrangements for joint sessions and joint meetings of the Congress, announcements of messages from the President and the Senate, announcement of the arrival of the President when he addresses Congress in person, escorting dignitaries visiting the Capitol—those are the tasks the public sees the Doorkeeper performing. In addition, he supervises the doormen stationed at each entrance to the House floor and House gallery; supervises the pages; operates the Document Room which provides copies of House bills, laws, committee reports and other documents to the Members, the media and the public on request. Under his jurisdiction are the staff members serving the media galleries and the Members' cloakrooms. He also distributes authorized publications such as the *Congressional Directory* and copies of the *U.S. Codes* to the Members and their staffs.

James T. Molloy, Doorkeeper.

James T. Molloy, Doorkeeper, with Ann Thornburg, his Administrative Assistant.

Postmaster of the House

The primary duty of the Postmaster is to provide mail pickup and delivery service to the House wing of the Capitol, the House office buildings and the House annexes. Four post offices are under his jurisdiction and provide the usual counter service.

The Postmaster also provides a mail security system which scans every piece of incoming mail. Over 50 million incoming letters and publications are processed annually. Another 50 million or more communications such as the *Congressional Record,* news releases, agency publications also are handled annually.

Robert V. Rota, Postmaster.

Postmaster of the House, Robert V. Rota, with Deputy Postmaster Nancy Auerbach, Administrative Assistant Joanna O'Rourke, Carlene Switzer and Barbara Straughan.

Chaplain of the House

The Chaplain is responsible for the opening prayer at each session of the House, and occasionally invites other clergy to serve as guest chaplains. The Chaplain's Office also coordinates use of the Prayer Room and makes arrangements for pastoral services for Members and staff.

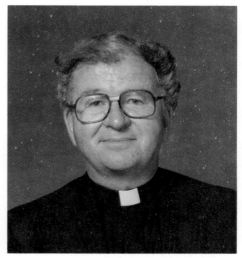

Reverend James D. Ford, Chaplain of the House.

The Reverend Dr. James Ford, Chaplain of the House, and his assistant, Sharman Brown, review the history of the Chaplaincy.

Donnald K. Anderson, Clerk of the House and W. Raymond Colley, Deputy Clerk.

The United States Senate

*Official portrait
of the United States,
April 9, 1987*

The Senate of the United States is the champion of the States and the co-equal partner of the House of Representatives. On the pediment of the Dirksen Senate Office Building are engraved in marble the words: "THE SENATE IS THE LIVING SYMBOL OF OUR UNION OF STATES."

There are 100 Senators, 2 from each of the States. They are elected for a term of 6 years by a rotating system of elections every 2 years so that "one-third may be chosen every second year". Fifteen times in its history, the Senate has proved to be a training ground for future Presidents of the United States.

The election of Senators by State legislatures, as originally provided in Article I of the Constitution, was abandoned in 1913 with the adoption of the 17th amendment, providing for direct vote by the people. The election of Senators by direct vote of the people associated the Senate more directly with the people and intensified the truly representative nature of the whole Congress. The Vice President of the United States, says the Constitution, "shall be President of the Senate, but shall have no vote, unless they be equally divided". Whether he wishes to vote or not in the event of such a tie, is a matter of choice with the Vice President himself.

The powers of the Senate overlap into the judicial and executive branches. Thus, the Senate is required to confirm most of the President's appointments. The Senate also approves or rejects treaties negotiated by the President with foreign powers. While the House has the power of impeachment, it is the Senate that tries officials who are impeached and has the aura and authority of a high court.

The Senate and the House enjoy the constitutional power to make their own rules of procedure. In fulfilling its legislative and informing functions, the Senate regulates debate by rules that are more fluid than the rules of the House. Any Senator may speak for as long as necessary except when debate is limited by the adoption of a cloture motion or by the terms of a unanimous consent agreement.

Bills in the process of becoming law may come to the Senate from the House or go to the House from the Senate. They are thus subject to the advantage of a second look. This doublecheck affords each legislative body a certain appellate function over the other.

A conference of committees of the two Houses generally works out a mutually acceptable compromise on a bill in controversy. Then, passed by both Houses in this final form, it is ready for submission to the President for his signature. Thereupon it becomes law.

This liaison between the two Houses produces deeply considered decisions. It brings to common ground the thinking of the House and the Senate. It develops cooperation.

The end result of this two-way scrutiny of prospective legislation is that it helps to cut to a minimum the margins for error and misjudgment.

Inherent in the bicameral system is the fundamental principle that no State, without its consent, shall be deprived of its equal suffrage in the Senate. Texas or Alaska, New York or California whether dominant in geography, in population, in natural resources or in financial power, cannot in the Senate overwhelm such States, for instance, as Rhode Island or Delaware, Mississippi or Montana or each other.

Senate Majority Leader Robert C. Byrd of West Virginia (right) and Senate Republican Leader Robert Dole of Kansas.

Senate Chamber Desks

When British troops set the Capitol ablaze in 1814, they heavily damaged the Senate Chamber and destroyed its furnishings. As part of the renovation to reopen the Chamber in 1819, the Senate ordered 48 desks at a cost of $34 each from Thomas Constantine, a New York cabinetmaker, who also built the desks for the House of Representatives. Many of these desks remain in the Senate Chamber today, and desks of a similar design have been added as each new State entered the Union.

Over the years several modifications have been made to the desks, primarily to provide more room for the Senators. During much of the 19th century a Senator's office was his desk on the Senate floor. Beginning in the 1830s 3-inch high mahogany writing boxes were added to the desks. Hinged on the top, these writing boxes opened to provide additional space.

Not all Senators preferred the modification, and today one desk still does not have a writing box. This is the Webster desk, which supposedly Daniel Webster refused to have altered on the grounds that, if his predecessor could have done without the additional space, so could he. None of Webster's successors have seen fit to abandon that stance. To match its height to the level of others in the Chamber, the desk is raised at its base. Webster had represented Massachusetts in the Senate but had been born in New Hampshire. For many years his desk was occupied by New Hampshire Senators Styles Bridges and Norris Cotton. In 1974, just before Cotton retired from the Senate, he secured adoption of a resolution (S. Res. 467, 93d Cong., 2d sess.) which required that the Webster desk always be assigned to the senior Senator from New Hampshire.

In the mid-19th century mahogany shelves were added at the base of the desks. Later at the turn of the century the legs of the desks were enclosed with a metal grille connected to a plenum chamber below the floor which provided better ventilation. The sanders and inkwells on top of the desks have also undergone change. The original inkwells were made from clear cut glass, covered with square, flat tops that moved horizontally. In 1933, what remained of the original inkwells were replaced by containers with hinged covers because duplicates of the earlier design were no longer being manufactured.

Over the years the desks have been rearranged periodically, as new States sent Senators and as party representation increased and diminished. When additional desks were needed, they were generally contracted out, although the last four desks, for Alaska in 1959 and Hawaii in 1960, were built in the Senate carpentry shop.

The easiest method for tracing the heritage of each desk is to read the names written and carved inside the desk drawers. This appears to be a 20th century tradition, since, for the most part, the earliest recorded names date back only to the first decade of the century. It is possible that 19th century Senators also inscribed their names in the desks, but that these names may have been lost during the refinishing of the drawers.

One difficulty in tracing back the names into the 19th century is that the early Senate Doorkeepers kept such information a closely guarded secret. Isaac Bassett, page and Doorkeeper from 1831 through 1895, feared that relic hunters might destroy the furniture if they knew which pieces were Clay's, Calhoun's and Webster's. Bassett had reasonable cause for alarm, for in 1861 he had stopped the mutilation of one of the Chamber's most famous desks. In April 1861, when the 6th Massachusetts Regiment was temporarily bivouacked in the Senate Chamber during a recess, Bassett entered the Chamber in time to hear the sound of splitting wood on the Democratic side. Rushing over he found a Union soldier bayonetting the desk vacated by Jefferson Davis, President of the Confederacy. "Stop that; stop that; what are you doing?" Bassett shouted. "That is not Jeff Davis' desk, it belongs to the Government of the United States. You were sent here to protect Government property, and not to destroy it." Today, a small block of wood inlaid on the left side of the desk (currently occupied by Senator John C. Stennis of Mississippi) covers the spot where the bayonet once struck.

The custom of dividing Senate desks by party is as old as the parties themselves, with Democrats traditionally sitting to the Presiding Officer's right and Republicans to his left. This division, however, has not always been so clear cut.

In the old Senate Chamber an equal number of desks were placed on either side of the aisle, without regard to party size. There was no hard rule as to placement, and during the 1840s and 1850s, some Democrats could be found sitting at random on the Whig side. When the Senate moved to its current Chamber in 1859 the practice of dividing the desks equally continued for several years.

The new Chamber was large enough to permit a more flexible seating arrangement, and in 1877 the practice developed of moving desks back and forth across the center aisle to permit all Members of the majority party to sit together on the appropriate side. From time to time since then, however, one party has elected such an overwhelming majority that it has again become necessary to have majority members sitting on the minority side. For instance, during the 60th Congress (1907–09) 10 Republicans sat on the Democratic side, while during the 75th Congress (1937–39) 13 Democrats sat on the Republican side.

Such seating became known as the "Cherokee Strip," meaning that the overflow of majority party Senators were off their reservation. (The Cherokee Strip in Oklahoma referred to land belonging to neither the Indian territory nor the states.)

The seating of the Majority and Minority leaders at the front row desks on either side of the center aisle is a relatively recent Senate tradition, dating back to 1927 for the Democrats and 1937 for the Republicans.

Daniel Webster's desk.

The Senate Majority Leader

*The Majority Leader
of the Senate is the closest
counterpart of the Speaker of
the House, although the
Framers of the Constitution
apparently did not foresee
such a development.*

The post of Majority Leader emerged and evolved during the twentieth century to meet both the political and institutional leadership needs of the Senate.

Selection

From 1789 through the end of the nineteenth century, the Senate operated without officially designated leaders. President Woodrow Wilson commented in 1885: "No one is *the* Senator. No one may speak for his party as well as himself." Leadership, instead, came from individual Members of the Senate, who exerted considerable personal influence, and from the chair-

men of powerful committees, who often led their party into legislative battle. In the late nineteenth century, the chairmen of the party caucuses played an increasingly important role in scheduling legislation on the Senate floor. By the early twentieth century, Democratic caucus minutes refer to the caucus chairman as the party's "official leader." However, not until 1920 did the Democrats officially designate a floor leader; the Republicans first used the term in 1925. At about the same time, the party leaders began the practice of sitting at the two front-row desks on either side of the center aisle in the Senate Chamber.

The Senate Majority
Leader and other
Congressional leaders
meet with the President
to discuss legislation.

The Senate Majority
Leader and the Senate
Republican Leader
after the official
exchange of
instruments on the INF
Treaty.

Today, the Majority and Minority Leaders are elected by a majority vote of all the Senators in their respective party conferences. The practice has been to choose the leaders for a two-year term at the beginning of each Congress.

Powers and Duties

The Majority Leader is the elected spokesman on the Senate floor for the majority party. Although certain powers are by custom and practice conferred on the Majority Leader, the office is essentially a political post.

The Legislative Reorganization Acts of 1946 and 1970, and subsequent revisions of the Senate rules, have given unique authority to the Majority Leader. The Leader is an integral part of the Senate's effective functioning, and is responsible for the enactment of the majority party's program. In addition to pending legislative matters, the Majority Leader must keep informed on national and international problems.

On the floor of the Senate, the Majority Leader is charged by his party members to deal with programmatic and scheduling matters in consultation with them and his party's policy-making bodies. The Leader keeps his party colleagues informed about proposed legislative actions on pending business. In recent years, the role of the Majority Leader in scheduling legislation has greatly increased.

The Majority Leader or his designee remains in the Chamber at all times when the Senate is in session to see that the program is carried out to the party's satisfaction. In the course of Senate activities, the Majority Leader (a) makes motions to proceed to the consideration of all proposed legislation (bills and resolutions); (b) proffers routine requests to accommodate the Senate, including orders to permit standing committees to meet while the Senate is in session; (c) offers motions to recess or adjourn from day to day; (d) determines what the daily schedule will be for the floor work; and (e) conducts the necessary parliamentary actions to expedite the Majority party's legislative program.

In earlier years, committee chairmen usually submitted motions to proceed to the consideration of bills reported from their own committees. At the present time, nearly all such motions are made by the Majority Leader.

The Majority Leader keeps in close touch with the Minority Leader as to proposed legislation to be brought up, the procedure to be followed, and the legislative contests to be staged.

Senate Majority Leader, Robert C. Byrd of West Virginia, with colleagues, Wendell H. Ford of Kentucky, Chairman of the Senate Committee on Rules and Administration, Daniel K. Inouye of Hawaii, Secretary of the Democratic Conference Committee, and Alan Cranston of California, Democratic Whip. This photograph was taken in the President's Room located in S–216 of the Capitol.

Biography in Brief of the Senate Majority Leader

A pensive Senate Majority Leader ponders the problems of the Nation—and the world.

A young Robert C. Byrd (right) helps carry lunch pails to the local boarding house in West Virginia.

In 1967, Senator Robert C. Byrd entered the Senate leadership, winning election as secretary of the Democratic Conference. Four years later, he became his party's whip—the number two Senate leadership position. In 1977, Senate Democrats unanimously elevated him to the post of Majority Leader. Since then, he has served continuously as his party's leader and is the only person in Senate history to have held, in succession, the posts of Majority Leader (1977–1981), Minority Leader (1981–1987), and Majority Leader (1987–1989).

Robert Carlyle Byrd was born Cornelius Calvin Sale, Jr., on November 20, 1917, in North Wilkesboro, North Carolina. His mother, Ada Kirby Sale, died in the 1918 influenza epidemic. In accordance with his wife's final wish, Cornelius Sale, a factory worker with four older children to raise, entrusted the baby to his sister Vlurma and her husband Titus Dalton Byrd, whose only child had died. They renamed their nephew Robert Carlyle Byrd and moved with him to West Virginia. There, young

Senator Byrd is frequently a spokesman for his party.

Robert's foster father held a succession of subsistence income jobs as brewery worker, farmer, and coal miner.

Raised in impoverished circumstances during the grimmest years of the Great Depression, Robert graduated as valedictorian of his high school class in May 1934, at the age of sixteen. He subsequently worked as a gas station attendant and then as a produce salesman in a mining company store. In 1937, he married his high school sweetheart, Erma Ora James, a coal miner's daughter. In the years prior to World War II, Robert Byrd taught himself the butcher's trade. During the war he labored as a welder in the shipyards of Baltimore, Maryland, and Tampa, Florida.

At war's end, he outdistanced a field of thirteen candidates in a 1946 Democratic primary and went on to win a seat in the West Virginia House of Delegates. In 1950, he was elected to the State senate. During that time, Robert Byrd opened a grocery store and pursued his undergraduate education at Beckley Junior College, Morris Harvey College, Marshall College, and Concord College. In 1952, deciding to campaign for an open seat in the U.S. House of Representatives, he won the general election by an impressive margin.

Robert C. Byrd was elected to the United States Senate in 1958, following three terms in the House. As a freshman Senator, he received a coveted appointment to the Appropriations Committee. Recognizing the value of legal training to Congressional service, Byrd, in 1953, had begun evening law school courses. A decade later, while in the Senate, he received his Doctor of Jurisprudence degree, *cum laude*, from American University's Washington College of Law, the only person ever to have begun and completed the studies leading to a law degree while serving in the Congress.

Senator Byrd holds a number of significant West Virginia political records. He has served longer in the Senate than any of the twenty-nine other Senators elected from that State. He is the only West Virginian to have served in both Chambers of the State legislature and in both Houses of the United States Congress. He also is the only public official of his State to have won a contested general election in all of its fifty-five counties (1970), and the only U.S. Senator ever elected without opposition in a West Virginia general election (1976). In his political career of forty-two years, he has never been defeated.

Senator and Mrs. Byrd have two daughters, Mona Fatemi and Marjorie Moore, and six grandchildren—Erik, Darius, and Fredrik Fatemi; and Mona and Mary Anne Moore (and Jon Michael Moore, deceased).

The Majority Leader is an expert parliamentarian, a skill he uses to advance the goals of his party. Here he testifies before a group seeking to investigate Senate rules and practices.

Senator Byrd plays the fiddle at a Democratic Dinner.

Senator Byrd greets British Prime Minister, Margaret Thatcher.

The Senate Majority Leader joins the President in greeting Soviet leader, Mikhail Gorbachev.

Graduate of American University law school.

Senator and Mrs. Byrd at their 50th wedding anniversary celebration.

Senator Byrd attends a reception at the Botanic Garden.

Former Senate Majority Leaders

Fourteen men have formally served as Majority Leader of the United States Senate since the emergence of the position in the 68th Congress. Of the 14 Majority Leaders, Alben W. Barkley, of Kentucky and Charles Curtis, of Kansas, later served as Vice Presidents, and Lyndon B. Johnson, of Texas, served as Vice President and President. Senator Mike Mansfield, of Montana, has the distinction of having the longest continuous service as Majority Leader, having served from January 3, 1961, until January 3, 1977, for a total of 16 years.

Senator Robert C. Byrd of West Virginia is the only person in Senate history to have held, in succession, the posts of Majority Leader (1977–1981), Minority Leader (1981–1987), and Majority Leader (1987–1989), and he has had the longest continuous service in party leadership posts (22 years).

Charles Curtis
of Kansas: the first to actually be called a "floor leader." Majority Leader, first session of the 68th Congress through the 70th Congress, from November 28, 1924 to March 3, 1929. Later served as Vice President of the United States.

James E. Watson
of Indiana: Majority Leader, 71st and 72nd Congresses, from March 5, 1929 to March 3, 1933.

Joseph T. Robinson
of Arkansas: Majority Leader, 73rd Congress through the first session of the 75th Congress, from March 4, 1933 to July 14, 1937.

Alben W. Barkley
of Kentucky: Majority Leader, 75th Congress, first session, through 79th Congress, July 22, 1937 to January 3, 1947. Later served as Vice President of the United States.

Wallace H. White, Jr.
of Maine: Majority Leader, 80th Congress, January 3, 1947 to January 3, 1949.

Scott W. Lucas
of Illinois: Majority Leader in the
81th Congress, January 20, 1949 to
January 3, 1951.

Ernest W. McFarland
of Arizona: Majority Leader, 82nd
Congress, February 22, 1951 to
January 3, 1953.

Robert A. Taft
of Ohio: Majority Leader in the
83rd Congress, first session, from
January 3, 1953 to July 31, 1953.

William F. Knowland
of California: Majority Leader in
the 83rd Congress, from August 4,
1953 to January 3, 1955.

Lyndon B. Johnson
of Texas: The former U.S.
President and Vice President
served as Majority Leader from the
84th through the 86th Congresses,
from January 3, 1955 to January 3,
1961. Later served as Vice
President and President of the
United States.

Mike Mansfield
of Montana: Majority leader from
the 87th through the 94th
Congresses, January 3, 1961 to
January 3, 1977. Now serving as
United States Ambassador to
Japan.

Robert C. Byrd
of West Virginia: Majority Leader
from the 95th Congress through
the 96th Congresses, January 3,
1977 to January 3, 1981; and in the
100th Congress, January 6, 1987 to
January 3, 1989.

Howard H. Baker, Jr.
of Tennessee: Majority Leader
from the 97th Congress through
the 98th Congress, January 3, 1981
to January 3, 1985.

Robert Dole
of Kansas: Majority Leader in the
99th Congress, January 3, 1985 to
January 6, 1987.

The Senate Republican Leader

Senate leadership is not a 9-to-5 job.

Bob Dole is one of America's best known and most respected leaders. During a distinguished Congressional career that spans almost 30 years, the Kansas Republican has held an impressive number of leadership posts, topped in 1984 when his Senate colleagues picked him to be their Majority Leader. Two years later, he was unanimously re-elected to be the Senate Republican Leader.

However, as a youngster growing up during the dust bowl years on the plains of Kansas, Bob Dole never considered a career in politics. A star high school athlete and scholar, he was set on becoming a doctor. But World War II interrupted those plans and forever changed his life.

On April 14, 1945, Second Lieutenant Dole was gravely wounded on an Italian battlefield as he led his platoon against heavily entrenched German forces. Trying to rescue one of his men, Dole was cut down in a hail of enemy fire.

What followed were 4 long, agonizing years in Army hospitals. Although he was paralyzed from the neck down, Bob Dole fought through all kinds of complications to not only walk again, but to set off on a journey that would take him to the pinnacle of power on Capitol Hill. It was a miraculous comeback that stunned the experts, although his war wounds cost him the use of his right arm.

Thanks to the G.I. Bill, he completed his education at Washburn University Law School in Topeka where he graduated with top honors. In fact, Senator Dole's political career began with a term in the Kansas House of Representatives while he was still a law student. In 1952, he was elected to the first of four terms as County Attorney in Russell, Kansas. Next, it was on to Washington for four consecutive terms in the U.S. House of Representatives. In 1968, the people of Kansas made him their newest Senator. Now in his

Senate leaders Dole and Byrd, plus Senator Pete Wilson, take it on the chin from the middleweight boxing champ Sugar Ray Leonard.

Bob and Elizabeth Dole.

1944—U.S. Army Camp Breckenridge, Kentucky: An athletic 194 pounds.

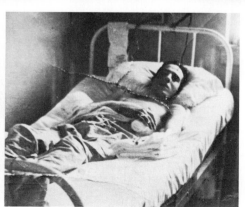

1945—Fighting for his life, a gravely wounded Second Lieutenant Bob Dole: 122 pounds.

fourth Senate term, Bob Dole demonstrated his tremendous popularity by winning every county in the 1980 and 1986 State elections.

The Senior Senator from Kansas first rose to national prominence in 1972 when he was named his party's national chairman, and again in 1976 as the Republican Vice-Presidential candidate with President Ford.

In 1980, the Kansas Senator became the chairman of the powerful Senate Finance Committee where he won plaudits for his leadership on the economy, Social Security, and programs for the disadvantaged. Often called the "Voice of Agriculture", Senator Dole has also been a towering figure on the House and Senate Agriculture Committees for 28 years.

Married to the equally dynamic Elizabeth Dole—President Reagan's former Transportation Secretary—the Doles make up one of the Nation's most attractive and powerful couples. The Senator has one daughter, Robin.

In constant demand as a speaker, Senator Dole is well-known for his sense of humor, which he prefers to turn on himself. He once summed up his view of public service in this way: "It is good that we laugh at ourselves or millions of others will do it for us. A dose of humility is welcome medicine."

On Board Air Force One, the President confers with his Senate Leader.

A dynamic speaker, Senator Dole announces for the Presidency, 1988.

When the Republican Leader speaks, the media listen.

Senator Dole remembers his fallen World War II comrades at an Italian cemetery.

Senator Dole travels the world to deliver America's message of Freedom and Democracy. He is pictured here in his famous confrontation with communist strongman, Daniel Ortega of Nicaragua.

Senate Leadership

The Constitution requires that the Vice President serve as the President of the Senate. Since the Vice President is frequently not present in the Senate, except in the case of a close vote which may end in a tie, the Senate elects a President pro tempore; by custom, in recent decades, the most senior majority party Member of the Senate. The President pro tempore is a key member of his party's policymaking body. He usually designates a more junior Senator to preside over daily sessions in his place. The President pro tempore also has the responsibility for the Office of the Legislative Counsel, a group of legal specialists who assist Senators in drafting bills.

Since the early days of the twentieth century, the Senate has, by custom, developed the position of Majority Leader as a parallel in power to the Speaker of the House.

The real leader of the Senate is the Majority Leader. He is the legisla-

Senate Democratic leadership for the 100th Congress: John C. Stennis of Mississippi, President pro tempore; Daniel K. Inouye of Hawaii, Secretary of the Democratic Conference; Alan Cranston of California, Democratic Whip; and Robert C. Byrd of West Virginia, Majority Leader.

Deputy President pro tempore of the Senate, George J. Mitchell of Maine.

The Chairman of the Democratic Senatorial Campaign Committee, John F. Kerry of Massachusetts.

tive strategist and exercises considerable influence on committee assignments.

The Majority Leader is elected by the Senators who are members of the political party to which more than 50 percent of the Senators belong. The Senators of the party with the lesser number elect a Minority Leader.

In cooperation with their party organization, each Leader is responsible for the achievement of the legislative program. They manage the order in which legislation moves to passage and expedite noncontroversial legislation. They keep members of their party informed regarding pending business. Each Leader is an ex-officio member of his party's policymaking and organizing body. Each is aided by an assistant leader, called the Whip, as in the House, and by the Majority or Minority Secretary, who are profes-

sional staff administrators, but not Members of the Senate.

The two major parties in the Senate are organized differently. The Democrats have a caucus which nominates the Leader, elects the Steering Committee and approves Steering Committee nominations for Committee Chairmen. The Steering Committee nominates Committee Chairmen and assigns party members to Committees. The Democratic Policy Committee develops legislative policy and positions.

The Republican Senators comprise the Republican Conference, which elects the Republican Leader and deals with procedural matters. The Conference Committee assigns party members to Committees. They also elect the Republican Policy Committee which handles the research and policy determination function of the party.

Senate Republican leadership of the 100th Congress: Bill Armstrong of Colorado, Chairman of the Republican Policy Committee; Thad Cochran of Mississippi, Secretary of the Senate Republican Conference; John H. Chafee of Rhode Island, Chairman of the Senate Republican Conference; Robert Dole of Kansas, Republican Leader; Strom Thurmond of South Carolina, Ranking Republican Member of the Senate; Alan K. Simpson of Wyoming, Republican Whip; and Rudy Boschwitz of Minnesota, Chairman of the National Republican Senatorial Committee.

Elected Officers of the Senate

At the beginning of each session the Senate elects its officers for a two year term. These officers are: the Secretary of the Senate, the Sergeant at Arms of the Senate, the Majority and Minority Secretaries of the Senate and the Chaplain of the Senate.

Secretary of the Senate

The primary duty of this officer is the legislative administration of the Senate. He is custodian of the Senate Seal; he administers oaths of office; certifies passage of legislation, as well as the ratification of treaties and confirmation or rejection of Presidential nominations. He is assisted in his legislative administration by a wide variety of experts, including the Parliamentarian, Legislative Clerk, Staff of the Office of Classified National Security Information, Journal Clerk, Disbursing Officer, Senate Librarian, Senate Historian and official reporters, among others. He also is a member of the Federal Election Commission, the Federal Council on the Arts and Humanities and serves as Executive Secretary to the Commission on Art and Antiquities of the Senate.

Sergeant at Arms of the Senate

The responsibility of the Sergeant at Arms of the Senate is primarily to enforce the rules of the Senate and maintain decorum. In addition he supervises the computer and micrographic centers, Senate post offices, press galleries, service department, recording studio, telephone services and janitorial services. He rotates with the House Sergeant at Arms as chairman of the Capitol Police Board and the Capitol Guide Board. He also is the protocol officer of the Senate, including the announcement of the arrival of the President and other dignitaries.

Henry Kuualoha Giugni, Sergeant at Arms.

Secretary of Senate, Walter J. (Joe) Stewart discusses matters of the Senate with his deputy, Jim English.

Walter J. (Joe) Stewart, Secretary of the Senate.

Secretaries to the Majority and the Minority

The Secretary to the Majority and the Secretary to the Minority are also elected officers of the Senate. Their duties are similar—primarily to supervise the majority and minority cloakrooms, obtain pair votes for Senators as requested, brief Senators on votes and issues under consideration, poll the Senators at the request of the leadership and, in general, serve the Senators who comprise the majority and minority.

C. Abbott (Abby) Saffold, Secretary to the Majority.

Howard O. Greene, Jr., Secretary to the Minority.

Chaplain of the Senate

The Chaplain of the Senate serves as pastor to the Senators and their families. He opens the sessions of the Senate each day with prayer. His office is a resource center for information concerning the Bible, various religious denominations and the subject of religion in general.

C. Abbott Saffold, Secretary to the Majority, and Robert A. Bean, Assistant Secretary to the Majority.

Howard O. Greene, Secretary to the Minority, and John L. Doney, Assistant Secretary to the Minority.

Chaplain Halverson checks his calendar with his assistant, Joan Crownover.

Reverend Richard C. Halverson, Chaplain of the Senate.

119

Five Outstanding Senators

Five outstanding Senators of the past were chosen by a Special Committee, and approved by the entire Senate.

Adjacent to the Senate Chamber on the second floor of the Senate wing of the Capitol is the Senate Reception Room.

Aside from "real live Senators" who leave the Senate floor to confer with constituents, government officials, lobbyists and visitors during sessions of the Senate, the most impressive feature of the Senate Reception Room is the series of portraits of five former U.S. Senators selected as outstanding among all the persons who served in the U.S. Senate before 1959, the year the portraits were placed in the five hitherto empty spaces.

Clay

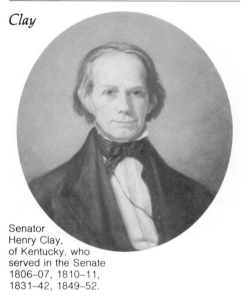

Senator
Henry Clay,
of Kentucky, who
served in the Senate
1806–07, 1810–11,
1831–42, 1849–52.

Webster

Senator
Daniel Webster,
of Massachusetts,
who served in the
Senate
1827–41, 1845–50.

Calhoun

Senator
John C. Calhoun,
of South Carolina, who
served in the Senate
1832–43, 1845–50.

La Follette

Senator
Robert M.
La Follette, Sr., of
Wisconsin,
who served in the
Senate 1906–25.

Taft

Senator
Robert A. Taft,
of Ohio, who served in
the Senate 1939–53.

A Special Senate Committee on the Senate Reception Room was established by a resolution of the 84th Congress. Senator John F. Kennedy (D–Massachusetts), was named Chairman. The other members of the committee were: Senators Richard B. Russell (D–Georgia), Mike Mansfield (D–Montana), John W. Bricker (R–Ohio) and Styles Bridges (R–New Hampshire). The committee was charged with the duty of selecting "five outstanding persons from among all persons, but not a living person, who have served as Members of the Senate since the formation of the Government of the United States whose paintings shall be placed in the five unfilled spaces in the Senate Reception Room."

Chairman John F. Kennedy was the chief organizer and proponent of the project to select the outstanding Senators. During long months of convalescence from back surgery to correct damage from injuries received in World War II, Senator Kennedy studied extensively the lives and contributions of great Americans who in times of decision placed the national good above popular opinion. His book, *Profiles in Courage,* was the forerunner of his work on the special committee. The Senate resolution also authorized the committee to consult with "historians and other sources, including the general public as it deems advisable."

The criteria recommended by the advisory committee provided that the five Senators should be chosen without regard for their services in other offices, that they should be distinguished for acts of statesmanship transcending party and state lines, and that their leadership in national thought and constitutional interpretation be considered as well as in legislation.

The committee reported on May 1, 1957. The report stressed that those selected were "not necessarily the five greatest Senators; nor the most blameless or irreproachable ones, nor models of contemporary behavior. Allowances must be made, moreover, of the times, the morals, and the practices of the period in which each served; and political and policy differences should not diminish their claim to the label outstanding."

The artists commissioned by the Senate were Arthur Conrad for Calhoun; Allyn Cox for Clay; Chester La Follette for La Follette; Dean C. Keller for Taft; and Adrian Lamb for Webster.

From left to right: Republican Whip Alan K. Simpson of Wyoming; Republican Leader Robert Dole of Kansas; Majority Leader Robert C. Byrd of West Virginia and Majority Whip Alan Cranston of California meet in the Senate Reception Room.

Vice President of the United States and President of the Senate

The Vice President, who is the constitutionally designated presiding officer of the Senate, is a unique figure in our Government. He is the only official with duties both in the executive and legislative branches. For many years the Vice President was not much more than "the man in the wings" waiting to fill the void should a vacancy occur in the Presidency.

Since Harry Truman's Presidency, however, the role of the Vice President has been steadily expanded, and now more than ever the Vice President does indeed play a key role in our system of Government.

The Constitution states the role of the President of the Senate as follows: "The Vice President of the United States shall be President of the Senate, but shall have no vote, unless they be equally divided." And again the Constitution stipulates: "The Senate shall chuse [sic] their other Officers, and also a President pro tempore, in the Absence of the Vice President, or when he shall exercise the Office of President of the United States."

George Herbert Walker Bush, of Texas, the 43rd man to serve as Vice President, is no stranger to the Capitol, having served in the U.S. House of Representatives for two terms. His father, the late Prescott Bush, served as U.S. Senator from Connecticut. The

Supreme Court Justice Potter Stewart administers the Oath of Office to the 44th Vice President of the United States, George Herbert Walker Bush, as Mrs. Barbara Bush holds the Bible. Photo by Senator Patrick J. Leahy.

The President and Vice President of the United States.

The President confers with his working Vice President. As did his predecessor, President Carter, President Reagan has made the Vice President a key leader in his administration.

U.S. Senate confirmed the appointments of the younger Bush as U.S. Ambassador to the United Nations in 1971 and as Director of the Central Intelligence Agency in 1976. He also served as Chief of the U.S. Liaison Office in the People's Republic of China in 1974–75.

He served from August 1942 to September 1945 as a naval aviation cadet and carrier pilot, and fought in the Pacific, winning three Air Medals and the Distinguished Flying Cross.

He is married to the former Barbara Pierce, of Rye, NY. They are the parents of five children and have two grandchildren.

The President and Vice President visit informally at the White House with Great Britain's Prime Minister, Margaret Thatcher.

The Vice President visits House Judiciary Committee Chairman, Peter W. Rodino, Jr. of New Jersey.

The Vice President with his wife, Barbara, in his ceremonial office near the Senate Chamber.

The Vice President and Senator Strom Thurmond of South Carolina chat with Mrs. Bush, who is in uniform as a participant in the traditional Senate Wives Red Cross production program.

As President of the Senate, the Vice President presides with the Speaker of the House at joint sessions of Congress.

Vice President Bush. Photograph by former Senator Howard H. Baker of Tennessee.

Vice President Bush confers with White House Chief of Staff Howard Baker.

Former Vice Presidents of the United States

Forty-two men have formerly served as Vice President of the United States. Of this total, thirteen later became Presidents of the United States. Forty white marble busts of Vice Presidents have been placed in the Senate wing of the Capitol. The first twenty busts were placed in the gallery niches of the Senate Chamber. One is in the Vice President's formal office and the remainder are in the second floor corridors immediately around the Senate Chamber. The bust of Walter Mondale will be placed in 1988 and that of Spiro Agnew has not yet been commissioned. Under each legend is listed the sculptor and date of purchase or commission of the bust.

John Adams,
Massachusetts; George Washington's Vice President (1789); second President of the United States.
Daniel Chester French 1890

Thomas Jefferson,
Virginia; Vice President under John Adams (1797); was elected third President of the United States.
Sir Moses Ezekiel 1889

Aaron Burr,
New York; Thomas Jefferson's Vice President (1801).
Jacques Jovenal 1893

George Clinton,
New York; Vice President (1805) in Thomas Jefferson's second term; served also as Vice President under James Madison (1809).
Vittorio A. Ciani 1894

Elbridge Gerry,
Massachusetts; Vice President (1813) under James Madison.
Herbert Adams 1892

Daniel D. Tompkins,
New York; Vice President (1817) under James Monroe.
Charles H. Niehaus 1891

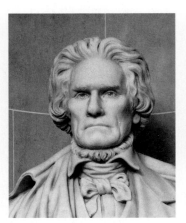

John C. Calhoun,
South Carolina; Vice President (1825) under John Q. Adams; reelected Vice President 1828 on the Jackson ticket.
Theodore A. Mills 1896

Martin Van Buren,
New York; Vice President under Andrew Jackson (1833); succeeded to Presidency in 1837.
U. S. J. Dunbar 1891

Richard M. Johnson,
Kentucky; Martin Van Buren's Vice President (1837).
James P. Voorhees 1895

John Tyler,
Virginia; William H. Harrison's Vice President (1841). Succeeding to Presidency same year.
William C. McCauslen 1898

George M. Dallas,
Pennsylvania; James K. Polk's Vice President (1845).
Henry J. Ellicott 1893

Millard Fillmore,
New York; Zachary Taylor's Vice President (1849), succeeding him to the Presidency when Taylor died.
Robert Cushing 1895

William R. King,
North Carolina and Alabama; Franklin Pierce's Vice President (1853).
William C. McCauslen 1896

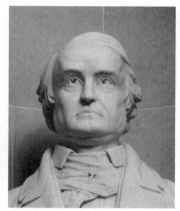

John C. Breckinridge,
Kentucky; James Buchanan's Vice President (1857).
James P. Voorhees 1896

Hannibal Hamlin,
Maine; Abraham Lincoln's Vice President (1861).
Franklin Simmons 1889

Andrew Johnson,
Tennessee; Abraham Lincoln's Vice President (1865); succeeded Lincoln on latter's death.
William C. McCauslen 1900

Schuyler Colfax,
Indiana; Ulysses S. Grant's Vice President (1869).
Frances M. Goodwin 1897

Henry Wilson,
New Hampshire and Massachusetts; Ulysses S. Grant's Vice President (1873).
Daniel Chester French 1885–86

William A. Wheeler,
New York; Rutherford B. Hayes' Vice President (1877).
Edward C. Potter 1892

Chester A. Arthur,
New York; James A. Garfield's Vice President (1881), succeeding to Presidency same year.
Augustus Saint-Gaudens 1892

Thomas A. Hendricks,
Ohio and Indiana; Grover
Cleveland's Vice President (1885).
U. S. J. Dunbar 1890

Levi P. Morton,
Vermont and New York; Benjamin
Harrison's Vice President (1889).
F. Edwin Elwell 1891

Adlai E. Stevenson,
Kentucky and Illinois; Grover
Cleveland's Vice President (1893).
Franklin Simmons 1894

Garret A. Hobart,
New Jersey; William McKinley's
Vice President (1897).
F. Edwin Elwell 1901

Theodore Roosevelt,
New York; William McKinley's
Vice President (1901);
26th President
of the United States.
James Earle Fraser 1910

Charles W. Fairbanks,
Ohio and Indiana; Theodore
Roosevelt's Vice President (1905).
Franklin Simmons 1909

James S. Sherman,
New York; William H. Taft's
Vice President (1909).
Bessie Potter Vonnoh 1912

Thomas R. Marshall,
Indiana; Woodrow Wilson's
Vice President (1913).
Moses A. Wainer Dykaar 1920

Calvin Coolidge,
Vermont and Massachusetts;
Warren G. Harding's Vice President
(1921); succeeded to Presidency,
1921.
Moses A. Wainer Dykaar 1929

Charles G. Dawes,
Ohio and Illinois; Calvin Coolidge's
Vice President (1925).
Jo Davidson 1935

Charles Curtis,
Kansas; Herbert C. Hoover's Vice
President (1929).
Moses A. Wainer Dykaar 1935

John Nance Garner,
Texas; Franklin Delano
Roosevelt's Vice President (1933).
James Earle Fraser 1943

Henry A Wallace,
Iowa; Franklin Delano Roosevelt's
Vice President (1941).
Jo Davidson 1948

Harry S. Truman,
Missouri; Franklin Delano
Roosevelt's Vice President (1945);
succeeded to Presidency.
Charles Keck 1947

Alben W. Barkley,
Kentucky; Harry S. Truman's Vice
President (1949).
Kalervo Kallio 1958

Richard Nixon,
California; Dwight D. Eisenhower's
Vice President (1953); President
of United States 1969–1972.
Gualberto Rocchi 1965

Lyndon B. Johnson,
Texas; John F. Kennedy's Vice
President (1961); succeeded to
Presidency.
Jimilu Mason 1966

Hubert H. Humphrey,
South Dakota and Minnesota;
Lyndon B. Johnson's Vice President
(1965).
Walker Hancock 1984

Sprio T. Agnew,
Maryland; Richard M. Nixon's Vice
President (1969).
Pending

Gerald R. Ford,
Nebraska and Michigan; Richard
M. Nixon's Vice President (1973);
President of the United States.
Charles Calverly 1985

Nelson A. Rockefeller,
Maine and New York; Gerald
R. Ford's Vice President (1974).
John Calabro 1987

Walter F. Mondale,
Minnesota; James Earl (Jimmy)
Carter's Vice President (1977).
Judson Nelson 1988

Pages checking
legislative calendar.

Serving the Members of the United States Congress is a cadre of young adults known as pages. They have been employed since the early Congresses. Today they include both males and females from across the Nation.

Pages are selected by Representatives and Senators whose seniority permits this privilege. Although the ages of pages have varied over the years between 14 and 18, they now must be at least juniors in high school.

Pages are appointed to serve in either the House of Representatives or the Senate and customarily serve the Members of their sponsors' party. However, they are available to assist any Member of the chamber to which they have been appointed.

The pages of the House and Senate serve principally as messengers carrying documents, letters and messages between the House and Senate, Members' offices, committees and the Library of Congress. They also prepare

the House and Senate Chambers for each day's business. These tasks include distributing copies of committee documents and legislation to be considered and distributing copies of the *Congressional Record,* which contains an account of the previous day's Congressional proceedings and debates.

House page duties are designated by job assignments and titles—bench pages, floor pages, documentarian pages, cloakroom pages, page overseer and Speaker's page. These positions are rotated periodically among the pages. Senate pages perform duties similar to their House counterparts, although their jobs are not categorized by function.

Pages serve one or two terms of an academic year and also during the summer months. Their tenure depends on ability, conduct, academic performance and their sponsors' term in office.

Until 1971 no female pages had ever been hired. The first Senate female pages were appointed in May 1971 by former Senators Jacob Javits of New York and Charles Percy of Illinois. Subsequently, former Speaker Carl Albert of Oklahoma appointed the first female House page in 1973. Today, female and minority pages are in an integral part of the page system.

Congress has provided for the formal education of the pages since 1947. Until the 1983–1984 school year there was one page school (located in the Library of Congress) which was staffed by employees of the District of Columbia School System.

However, beginning in 1983, the House of Representatives opened its own House Page School. Located in the Library of Congress, this school has six teachers, a principal, and an administrative assistant, all of whom are employed by the House of Representatives.

The Senate Page School, also located in the Library of Congress, still educates its pages with District of Columbia teachers. It has six teachers, one of whom is a program coordinator, and an administrative assistant.

Senator David H. Pryor
of Arkansas

Senator Christopher J.
Dodd of Connecticut

Representative John D.
Dingell, Jr. of Michigan

Representative Bill
Emerson of Missouri

Representative Douglas
H. Bosco of California

Representative Paul E.
Kanjorski of
Pennsylvania

Representative Jim
Kolbe of Arizona

The curriculum of both schools is geared toward college preparation, and both offer courses which utilize the resources of Washington, D.C. Educational, recreational and social extracurricula activities are also available.

The classes of both schools usually meet in the morning (around 6:15 A.M.) prior to the convening of the House and Senate. The schedules may vary, however, with changes in the Congressional schedules.

Congress has provided supervised housing for the pages since 1983. The third and fourth floors of House Office Building Annex No. 1 were renovated for use as a page residential facility. It can accommodate 96 pages. Male and female pages are housed on different floors.

The residence hall has a full-time director and five proctors, all of whom are required to live in the facility. Generally, all pages are required to live in the hall. The cost for the residence, including an evening meal five days a week, is deducted from the pages' salaries each month and placed in a page revolving fund for the residence and meal plan. Security at the facility is provided 24 hours a day by the U.S. Capitol Police.

Several Members of Congress, as well as Congressional and Government officials, began their careers as Congressional pages. Former pages who are currently Members of the House are Representatives John Dingell, Jr., of Michigan, Bill Emerson of Missouri, Douglas Bosco of California, Paul Kanjorski of Pennsylvania, and Jim Kolbe of Arizona. Current Senators who are former pages are Senators David Pryor of Arkansas and Christopher Dodd of Connecticut, both of whom also served in the House of Representatives.

Moreover, Donnald K. Anderson, Clerk of the House, and Walter J. (Joe) Stewart, Secretary of the Senate, also served as Congressional pages.

Pages receiving their assignments.

The 1988 graduating class on the Capitol steps with House Speaker Jim Wright.

Pages in the House Cloakroom receiving instructions.

Pages sorting United States flags which flew over the Capitol.

Senate Majority Leader Robert C. Byrd of West Virginia (right), with Walter (Joe) Stewart, Secretary of the Senate and pages in Senate Cloakroom.

Your Congress at Work

The east central pediment of the Capitol showing the marble carving *Genius of America*.

A view of the Capitol by world renowned photographer, Fred J. Maroon, taken from the Washington Monument.

Members of Congress are as diverse as the States and districts they represent. They reflect the pluralistic nature of our society.

The Congress is composed of 540 individuals from our 50 States, as well as the District of Columbia, Puerto Rico, Guam, the Virgin Islands, and American Samoa. Like the American people they represent, each Member of Congress is different, yet each shares many similar traits. The following information indicates some of the common characteristics of our Representatives and Senators.

Age

The average age of Members of the 100th Congress is 51.4. The average age of Members of the House of Representatives is 50.7, and the average age of Members of the Senate is 54.4.

Representatives must be at least 25 when they take office. The youngest Representative is freshman John Rowland, Republican of Connecticut, who is 31. The oldest Representative is Claude Pepper, Democrat of Florida, who is 87.

Senators must be at least 30 when they take office. The youngest Senator is David Karnes, Republican of Nebraska. At 39, he is six days younger than Don Nickles, Republican of Oklahoma, and several months younger than Albert Gore, Democrat of Tennessee, and Kent Conrad, Democrat of North Dakota, all of whom were born in 1948. The oldest Senator is John Stennis, Democrat of Mississippi, who is 87.

Occupations

As has been true in previous Congresses, law is the dominant pro-

Representative John Rowland of Connecticut, youngest Member of Congress at age 31, confers with Navy personnel.

fession in the 100th Congress. There are presently 247 Members who have listed law as their profession. There are 170 Members with a business or banking background, 50 educators, 25 Members with backgrounds in agriculture, 28 with a journalism background, five engineers, three clergymen, one medical doctor, one dentist, one pharmacist, one optometrist and one veterinarian. Moreover, there are 16 former Governors, some 60 Members who are former Congressional staffers, six who were professional athletes, one who was an actor, two Members who were commercial airline pilots and one who was an astronaut.

Religion

During the last decade the number of Members of Congress

Senator Carl Levin and his brother, Representative Sander M. Levin, both of Michigan, have served together in Congress for over five years.

Senator John Stennis of Mississippi, President Pro Tempore of the Senate, is the oldest Senator at age 87.

identifying with one religious denomination or another has remained well over 90 percent. More than 500 Members of the 100th Congress cite a specific religious affiliation.

Although Protestants of various denominations collectively hold more seats in the 100th Congress than any other religious group, Roman Catholics, with 143 Members in the two Houses, make up the largest contingent of any one denomination. Of the Protestants, there are 76 Methodists, 60 Episcopalians, 57 Presbyterians, 52 Baptists and 23 Lutherans. There are 35 Jewish Members of Congress and smaller numbers of members of other religious groups.

Education

The Members of the 100th Congress are highly educated. There are at least 360 Representatives and 90 Senators with bachelor's degrees, 86 Representatives and 18 Senators with master's degrees, 186 Representatives and 64 Senators with law degrees, 14 Representatives and three Senators with doctoral degrees, two Representatives with medical degrees and one Senator with a veterinary medicine degree. In addition, five Senators and two Representatives are former Rhodes Scholars.

Congressional Service

The average length of service of Representatives in the 100th Congress is 9.25 years, about four and one-half terms. Representatives are elected for two-year terms. Representative Jamie Whitten, Democrat of Mississippi, has served longer in the House than any other Member of the 100th Congress

and is the Dean of the House. His service began on November 4, 1941.

The average length of service of Senators in the 100th Congress is 9.69 years, about one and one half terms. Senators are elected for six-year terms. Senator John Stennis, Democrat of Mississippi, has served longer in the Senate than any other Member of the 100th Congress. His service began on November 5, 1947.

Sex and Race

There are 25 women serving in the 100th Congress—two Senators and 23 Representatives. This is the same number as the 99th Congress, which had the largest number of women to serve in any Congress. There are 23 black Members of the 100th Congress (including one Delegate), all serving in the House of Representatives. This is the largest number of black Members to serve in any one Congress.

There are also 14 Hispanic Members of the 100th Congress (including three Delegates), eight Members (including two Delegates) who are of Asian/Pacific Island ancestry, and one Native American.

Representative Claude Pepper of Florida, the oldest Member of Congress at age 87. He is also the only Member who first served in the Senate and later in the House.

Tennessee's Senator Albert Gore, Jr., greets his mother and father, former Senator Albert Gore, Sr.

Women in American Politics

November 9, 1916, is a milestone in the history of the Nation. On that date Jeannette Rankin became the first woman elected to Congress. She was elected as Montana's Representative at-large to the House of Representatives. This occurred nearly four years before most women were given the right to vote. Since that time 123 other women have been elected or appointed to Congress.

Jeannette Rankin, an ardent suffragist, was elected to the 65th Congress in 1916, becoming the first woman Member of the House; and was elected again to the 77th Congress in 1941. During her two separate terms, Congress declared war (1917 and 1941), and thus she became the only Representative to vote against both declarations. Her statue was unveiled in Statuary Hall on May 1, 1985.

Jeannette Rankin served twice in the House; during the 65th Congress (1917–19) and during the 77th Congress (1941–43). Each time she voted against the declaration of war. In 1941 she was the only Member of Congress to do so, and she is the only person to have voted against U.S. entry into both World Wars.

There have been 110 women elected to the House of Representatives. Of these, 32 were elected to fill vacancies caused by the death of their husbands, and 13 of the 32 have subsequently been elected to additional terms. One woman, Winnifred Mason Huck of Illinois, was elected in 1922 to complete the term of her father who died in office.

Edith Nourse Rogers of Massachusetts holds the record for longevity of service by women in the House (35 years). She was elected to fill the vacancy caused by the death of her husband and served from June 25, 1925, until her death on September 10, 1960.

There have been 16 women elected or appointed to the Senate. Of these, 12 were first elected or appointed to fill unexpired terms. Seven of the 12 were elected or appointed to fill vacancies caused by the death of their husbands. Of the seven, two were subsequently elected to additional terms. They were Hattie Caraway of Arkansas and Maurine Neuberger of Oregon.

Margaret Chase Smith of Maine and Barbara Mikulski of Maryland are the only women to have served in both Houses. Moreover, Senator Smith was the first Republican woman elected to the Senate in her own right, and Senator Mikulski is the first and only woman in the Democratic party elected to the Senate in her own right.

Senator Smith was first elected to the House to fill the vacancy caused by the death of her husband and served from June 10, 1940, until January 3, 1949, when she began her Senate service. When she left the Senate on January 3, 1973, she had served there longer than any other woman (24 years), a record she still holds.

Senator Mikulski served in the House of Representatives from the 95th through the 99th Congresses (1977–87). In 1986, she was elected to the Senate.

Rebecca Latimer Felton of Georgia was the first woman to serve in the Senate. She was appointed in 1922 to complete the term of a Senator who had died in office. In addition to being the first woman Senator, Ms. Felton holds two other Senate records. Her tenure in the Senate has been the shortest ever (one day), and at the age of 87 she was the oldest person ever to begin Senate service.

Nancy Landon Kassebaum of Kansas and Paula Hawkins of Florida were the first women elected to the Senate without having first been elected or appointed to fill an unexpired term or elected first to the House of Representatives. Senator Kassebaum has served in the Senate since 1979 (96th Congress). Senator Hawkins served in the 97th through 99th Congresses (1981–87).

Suffragists picket the White House, January 1917.

The Sewell-Belmont House, home of the National Woman's Party, is located near the two newest Senate office buildings. It was declared a National Historic Site by act of Congress in 1975 in recognition of the women's suffrage movement.

During the War of 1812, the only shots fired against the British troops who burned the Capitol were fired from this house. Secretary of the Treasury Gallatin resided here during the development and signing of the Louisiana Purchase.

Visitors are welcomed each weekday from 10 a.m. to 2 p.m.; and noon to 4 p.m., Saturday and Sunday.

Senators Kassebaum and Mikulski are among only six women who have been elected to full six-year Senate terms. The others were Paula Hawkins, Margaret Chase Smith, Maurine Neuberger, and Hattie Caraway, the first woman elected to a full six-year term. Mrs. Caraway had first been appointed in 1931 to fill the vacancy caused by the death of her husband and was subsequently elected to her own terms. She served until January 1945.

Five women elected to Congress, all to the House, have been black. The first was Shirley Chisholm of New York who served from 1969–1983. The others were Yvonne Braithwaite Burke of California, Barbara Jordan of Texas, Katie Hall of Indiana, and Cardiss Collins of Illinois, the former chairwoman of the Congressional Black Caucus and a Member of the 100th Congress.

Representative Burke has been the only Member of Congress to give birth while in office. Her daughter, Autumn, was born in November 1973 during the 93d Congress (1973–75).

Seven women, to date, have chaired congressional committees. They were Senator Hattie W. Caraway and Representatives Martha W. Griffiths, Mae Ella Nolan, Mary T. Norton, Caroline L. O'Day, Leonor K. Sullivan and Edith N. Rogers.

There are 25 women in the 100th Congress—two Senators and 23 Representatives. This is the same number as the 99th Congress, which had the largest number of women to serve in any Congress.

Memorial to the Pioneers of the Women's Suffrage Movement.

This portrait monument of Elizabeth Cady Stanton, Susan B. Anthony and Lucretia Mott was accepted as a gift from the women of the United States, through the National Woman's Party, by the Joint Committee on the Library, February 15, 1921. The original block of marble from which these busts were carved measured 7' x 5'8" x 5', and the estimated weight is between 7 and 8 tons.

In accepting the monument the Joint Committee on the Library directed that it be placed temporarily "in the rotunda for the purpose of appropriate ceremonies of tender and reception and at the conclusion of the ceremonies, the said sculpture be placed in the crypt on the first floor of the Capitol beneath the dome." It was moved from the rotunda to the crypt May 1921.

Courtesy of the National Woman's Party.

Woman leaves jail after six-day hunger strike in abandoned Occoquan workhouse after her arrest on criminal charge of picketing the White House.

Suffragists march for voting rights parade near Capitol grounds, 1918.

Senators Nancy Kassebaum of Kansas and Barbara Mikulski of Maryland, the two women serving in the Senate during the 100th Congress.

A statue of Jeannette Rankin was given to the Congress by the Montana Historical Society in 1985.

(House wing, first floor of the Capitol)

Dedication of the Jeannette Rankin statue: Senator Max Baucus, Montana Governor Ted Schwinden, Sculptress Terry Mimnaugh, Former Speaker Thomas P. "Tip" O'Neill, Jr., Representative Ron Marlenee, Tom Kinney, representative of the Rankin family, Senator John Melcher, and Representative Pat Williams.

Representative Olympia Snowe of Maine, Pat Schroeder of Colorado, and Jan Meyers of Kansas in the Congresswomen's Suite House wing, first floor of the Capitol.

The Congress Represents You

Representative Norm Dicks of Washington introduces Budget Committee Chairman William H. Gray III of Pennsylvania to constituents on the Capitol steps.

Representative Ben Nighthorse Campbell of Colorado, a Northern Cheyenne Chief and the only Native American in the U.S. Congress, in traditional attire, riding his horse, Scamp.

Representative Thomas J. Downey of New York learns to draw—on a computer.

Senator John Glenn of Ohio greets the All-Ohio Youth Choir at the Ohio State Fair.

Representative James H. Quillen of Tennessee and constituent, Dolly Parton, at the dedication ceremony for the Dollywood Foundation in Pigeon Forge, Tennessee.

Senator Inouye receives floral lei from one of his constituents in Honolulu.

Representatives Duncan Hunter of California (left) discusses ship repair with San Diego Ship Repair Association President, Art Wardwell.

Oklahoma Senator David Boren (standing, center) and former Speaker of the House, Carl Albert, meet with summer interns.

Senator Orrin Hatch of Utah discusses the Constitution with attentive students.

Maryland Representative Beverly Byron takes a shot at celebrating the groundbreaking of the final leg of the National Freeway in May, 1987.

Maine Senator George J. Mitchell (standing, center) with Bangor-Brewer Middle School students on the Capitol steps.

Former President Gerald Ford confers with Indiana Senator Richard G. Lugar.

Representative Helen Delich Bentley of Maryland waves after christening the *Pride of Baltimore II*. Mrs. Bentley is the former Chairman of the Federal Maritime Commission.

The family of the late Senator Henry M. (Scoop) Jackson of Washington proudly display the Medal of Freedom posthumously awarded to Senator Jackson by President Reagan in June 1984. Left to right: daughter Anna Marie Jackson, wife, Helen Jackson and son Peter Jackson.

Speaker Jim Wright of Texas, a former Golden Gloves boxer, greets Sugar Ray Leonard, retired World Middle Weight Champion.

Santa Claus (a.k.a. Senator Howell Heflin of Alabama) is aided by helpers Senators Wendell Ford of Kentucky and John Warner of Virginia at the Senate Staff Club family Christmas party. The U.S. Marine Corps received thousands of dollars worth of toys for their annual ''Toys for Tots'' project.

Representative Patricia Schroeder of Colorado confers with constituent on mental health issues.

Senator Quentin Burdick of North Dakota (second from right) temporarily yields his seat to a future North Dakota voter.

Members of the U.S. Olympics Team meet with Representative Frank Annunzio of Illinois to thank him for introducing legislation to mint special commemorative coins which are expected to raise over $100 million for the support of the Olympics.

America's Cup skipper Dennis Conner is greeted by California Representative Bill Lowery and his wife, Kay, at a reception they held in his honor at the Navy Yard Museum in Washington, D.C.

Representative Pat Roberts (left) and Senator Nancy Landon Kassebaum, both of Kansas, confer with L. William Seidman, Chairman of the Federal Deposit Insurance Corporation.

California Representative Robert Badham meets with young constituents.

Interns proudly pose with their sponsor, Senator Malcolm Wallop of Wyoming.

Senators Max Baucus and John Melcher at Montana State Society reception in their honor, with President Debra Johnson and Vice President Rev. Jacob Beck.

Senator James A. McClure of Idaho visits with Boise senior citizens.

Partisan rivalries run high at the annual Congressional baseball game. Former Republican manager, Silvio O. Conte of Massachusetts, faces off Democratic opponent, Marty Russo of Illinois.

Senator John F. Kerry of Massachusetts makes a point to a senior citizen delegation.

Senator Ernest F. (Fritz) Hollings gets the word from constituents in Orangeburg, South Carolina.

Mississippians visit their Senator, Thad Cochran, in his Washington office.

Representative Mel Levine of California carries the Olympic torch across the Capitol grounds on its global journey to Calgary, Canada for the 1988 Winter Olympics.

Senator Warner of Virginia greets summer interns in his Washington office.

Representative Michel of Illinois with constituents from Peoria.

Senator Terry Sanford of North Carolina and wife, Margaret Rose, greet Bill Cochrane, constituent and long-time Senate staffer.

Senator Joseph Biden of Delaware, announces his candidacy for President of the United States in the rotunda of the Russell Senate Building.

Representative Jack Brooks of Texas, with his wife, Charlotte, at the unveiling of his official portrait in the House Committee on Government Operations.

Senator Rudy Boschwitz talks to constituents in his home state of Minnesota.

Senate Agriculture Committee Chairman, Pat Leahy, with Senate Republican Leader Dole. Senator Leahy is the best known photographer among Senators.

Representative Dan Glickman of Kansas meets with constituents.

CBS news correspondent, Leslie Stahl, interviews Representative Dick Cheney of Wyoming, and Senator George Mitchell of Maine.

Representative Ronald V. Dellums of California, left, and Representative Cardiss Collins of Illinois meet with Alex Haley, author of *Roots,* during a visit to the Capitol.

145

The Committee System

Representative Joseph Gaydos of Pennsylvania and Jim Abernathy of the Committee on House Administration staff.

"Congress in its committee rooms is Congress at work," wrote Woodrow Wilson. It is in the committees of Congress that bills undergo their closest scrutiny, that investigations—including oversight of the executive branch—are conducted, and that the differences in bills passed by each body are reconciled into one version acceptable to both.

Congress uses four distinct types of committees to perform these different functions: standing committees, select or special committees, joint committees and conference committees.

Committees that continue from Congress to Congress and formulate policy in designated areas are called standing committees. The subject jurisdictions of these permanent committees are set forth in the rules of each body, and virtually every introduced bill is referred to one or more of them according to the subjects involved. These are the committees that actually review proposed legislation and determine which bills shall be reported to each body.

In the 100th Congress there are 22 standing committees in the House and 16 in the Senate. Most have several subcommittees that address specified areas within the parent committee's jurisdiction. Usually a standing committee sends a bill to one of its subcommittees for initial scrutiny, including hearings and amendments. The bill is then reported to the full committee for consideration. Finally, if approved by the full committee, the bill is reported to the full House or Senate.

Standing committees also are responsible for overseeing the operations of the executive departments and agencies under their respective jurisdictions. They usually perform this function by means of studies which provide Congress with the facts necessary to determine whether the agencies are administering legislation as intended. Congressional studies also help committees identify areas in which legislative action might be needed and the form that action might take.

Other Congressional studies are

Members of the Senate Armed Services Committee.

performed by select or special committees. Usually established for a limited period of time, these groups ordinarily deal with more specific subjects and issues than do the standing committees. For example, each Chamber has a select or special committee on aging to study the multitude of problems that affect senior citizens. During the past decade each body has used a select committee to study its own committee system and to recommend improvements. Most select committees may investigate, study and make recommendations but may not report legislation. But both bodies have created a few permanent select committees in recent years and have authorized them to report legislation.

Congress uses joint committees for study and administrative purposes. These are usually permanent bodies composed of an equal number of House and Senate Members. Although in the past certain joint committees had the authority to consider and to report legislation, none of the four joint committees in the 100th Congress has this power. Usually joint committees are used to study broad

Meeting of the Members of the Joint Committee on Printing.

Photo courtesy of James F. Ashe/Time Magazine

Lt. Col. Oliver North taking the oath before select House and Senate committees investigating the Iran-Contra affair. The hearings were held in the historic Senate Caucus Room in the Russell Senate Office Building.

Senators Bob Dole of Kansas and Jesse Helms of North Carolina hear testimony before the Agriculture Committee.

and complex areas of interest to the entire Congress. For example, the Joint Committee on Printing sets policy for the printing and distribution of Federal publications and information to the Congress and the public.

The last category of committees is the conference committee. Conference committees are a means of reconciling the differences between the House and Senate when each passes a different version of the same bill. Conference committees are ad hoc joint committees; they are temporary panels appointed to deal with a single piece of legislation and they dissolve upon the completion of that task. Members of the House and Senate serve on each conference committee, and the number of Members from the two Chambers may differ. This is not as inequitable as it might seem because each Chamber's conferees get one vote; decisions must be approved by a majority of the Representatives and a majority of the Senators on the committee.

A lighter moment is shared between Senators David Boren of Oklahoma and Robert C. Byrd of West Virginia.

Senators J. Bennett Johnston of Louisiana and Quentin Burdick of North Dakota discuss an appropriations bill during a mark-up session.

Representative Jack Brooks, Chairman of the Committee on Government Operations, and Representative Frank Horton of New York, Ranking Minority Member.

MR. BROOKS CHAIRMAN

Every Member of the House serves on at least one committee except the Speaker and the Minority Leader who, by tradition, serve on none. Senators must serve on at least two committees. In the House, approximately 60 Representatives have only one committee assignment, usually because they sit on a particularly busy panel such as Appropriations. In general, however, House Members sit on three committees and Senators sit on four. In one way or another both bodies limit the number of chairmanships any single Member may hold.

Committee sizes vary considerably and sometimes change from Congress to Congress. Because the House has more than four times as many Members as the Senate, its committees generally are larger. In the 100th Congress the largest House Committee—Appropriations—has 57 members, and the largest Senate committee—also Appropriations—has 29. Most Senate standing committees have from 14 to 20 members, and most House ones have from 34 to 45. Traditionally party ratios on committees correspond roughly to the party ratio in the full Chamber.

Once assigned to a committee, a Member tends to return to that panel each Congress, thus specializing in and becoming expert on the committee's subject matters. The committee system continually builds up a reservoir of expertise to guide Congress as it deals with the Nation's needs.

The Senate Rules and Administration Committee oversees the day-to-day operations of the Senate. Ranking Republican Member, Ted Stevens of Alaska, and Chairman Wendell H. Ford of Kentucky listen to testimony.

Senator John Melcher of Montana speaking about the issues faced by senior citizens. He chairs the Senate Select Committee on Aging.

Members of the House Veterans Affairs Committee witness the Speaker's signature of an enrolled bill.

Committee Leadership of the 100th Congress

Standing Committees of the United States Senate

Armed Services

Chairman,
Sam Nunn
Georgia

Ranking Minority
Member,
John W. Warner
Virginia

Agriculture, Nutrition, and Forestry

Chairman,
Patrick J. Leahy
Vermont

Ranking Minority
Member,
Richard G. Lugar
Indiana

Banking, Housing, and Urban Affairs

Chairman,
William Proxmire
Wisconsin

Ranking Minority
Member,
Jake Garn
Utah

Appropriations

Chairman,
John C. Stennis
Mississippi

Ranking Minority
Member,
Mark O. Hatfield
Oregon

Budget

Chairman,
Lawton Chiles
Florida

Ranking Minority
Member,
Pete V. Domenici
New Mexico

Commerce, Science, and Transportation

Chairman,
Ernest F. Hollings
South Carolina

Ranking Minority
Member,
John C. Danforth
Missouri

Foreign Relations

Chairman,
Claiborne Pell
Rhode Island

Ranking Minority
Member,
Jesse Helms
North Carolina

Rules and Administration

Chairman,
Wendell H. Ford
Kentucky

Ranking Minority
Member,
Ted Stevens
Alaska

Energy and Natural Resources

Chairman,
J. Bennett Johnston
Louisiana

Ranking Minority
Member,
James A. McClure
Idaho

Governmental Affairs

Chairman,
John Glenn
Ohio

Ranking Minority
Member,
William V. Roth, Jr.
Delaware

Small Business

Chairman,
Dale Bumpers
Arkansas

Ranking Minority
Member,
Lowell P. Weicker, Jr.
Connecticut

Environment and Public Works

Chairman,
Quentin N. Burdick
North Dakota

Ranking Minority
Member,
Robert T. Stafford
Vermont

Judiciary

Chairman,
Joseph R. Biden, Jr.
Delaware

Ranking Minority
Member,
Strom Thurmond
South Carolina

Veterans' Affairs

Chairman,
Alan Cranston
California

Ranking Minority
Member,
Frank H. Murkowski
Alaska

Finance

Chairman,
Lloyd Bentsen
Texas

Ranking Minority
Member,
Bob Packwood
Oregon

Labor and Human Resources

Chairman,
Edward M. Kennedy
Massachusetts

Ranking Minority
Member,
Orrin G. Hatch
Utah

Select and Special Committees of the United States Senate

Aging

Chairman,
John Melcher
Montana

Ranking Minority
Member,
John Heinz
Pennsylvania

Indian Affairs

Chairman,
Daniel K. Inouye
Hawaii

Ranking Minority
Member,
Daniel J. Evans
Washington

Ethics

Chairman,
Howell T. Heflin
Alabama

Ranking Minority
Member,
Warren B. Rudman
New Hampshire

Intelligence

Chairman,
David L. Boren
Oklahoma

Vice Chairman,
William S. Cohen
Maine

Standing Committees of the United States House of Representatives

Appropriations

Chairman,
Jamie L. Whitten
Mississippi

Ranking Minority
Member,
Silvio O. Conte
Massachusetts

Banking, Finance and Urban Affairs

Chairman,
Fernand J. St Germain
Rhode Island

Ranking Minority
Member,
Chalmers P. Wylie
Ohio

Agriculture

Chairman,
E (Kika) de la Garza
Texas

Ranking Minority
Member,
Edward R. Madigan
Illinois

Armed Services

Chairman,
Les Aspin
Wisconsin

Ranking Minority
Member,
William L. Dickinson
Alabama

Budget

Chairman,
William H. Gray, III
Pennsylvania

Ranking Minority
Member,
Delbert L. Latta
Ohio

District of Columbia

Chairman,
Ronald V. Dellums
California

Ranking Minority
Member,
Stan Parris
Virginia

Government Operations

Chairman,
Jack Brooks
Texas

Ranking Minority
Member,
Frank Horton
New York

Merchant Marine and Fisheries

Chairman,
Walter B. Jones
North Carolina

Ranking Minority
Member,
Robert W. Davis
Michigan

Education and Labor

Chairman,
Augustus F. Hawkins
California

Ranking Minority
Member,
James M. Jeffords
Vermont

House Administration

Chairman,
Frank Annunzio
Illinois

Ranking Minority
Member,
Bill Frenzel
Minnesota

Post Office and Civil Service

Chairman,
William D. Ford
Michigan

Ranking Minority
Member,
Gene Taylor
Missouri

Energy and Commerce

Chairman,
Johh D. Dingell
Michigan

Ranking Minority
Member,
Norman F. Lent
New York

Interior and Insular Affairs

Chairman,
Morris K. Udall
Arizona

Ranking Minority
Member,
Don Young
Alaska

Public Works and Transportation

Chairman,
Glenn M. Anderson
California

Ranking Minority
Member,
John Paul
Hammerschmidt
Arkansas

Foreign Affairs

Chairman,
Dante B. Fascell
Florida

Ranking Minority
Member,
Wm. S. Broomfield
Michigan

Judiciary

Chairman,
Peter W. Rodino, Jr.
New Jersey

Ranking Minority
Member,
Hamilton Fish, Jr.
New York

Rules

Chairman,
Claude Pepper
Florida

Ranking Minority
Member,
James H. (Jimmy)
Quillen
Tennessee

Small Business

Chairman,
John J. LaFalce
New York

Ranking Minority
Member,
Joseph M. McDade
Pennsylvania

Veterans' Affairs

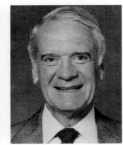

Chairman,
G.V. (Sonny)
Montgomery
Mississippi

Ranking Minority
Member,
Gerald B.H. Solomon
New York

Science, Space, and Technology

Chairman,
Robert A. Roe
New Jersey

Ranking Minority
Member,
Manuel Lujan, Jr.
New Mexico

Standards of Official Conduct

Chairman,
Julian C. Dixon
California

Ranking Minority
Member,
Floyd Spence
South Carolina

Ways and Means

Chairman,
Dan Rostenkowski
Illinois

Ranking Minority
Member,
John J. Duncan
Tennessee

Select Committees of the United States House of Representatives

Children, Youth, and Families

Chairman,
George Miller
California

Ranking Minority
Member,
Dan Coats
Indiana

Intelligence

Chairman,
Louis Stokes
Ohio

Ranking Minority
Member,
Henry J. Hyde
Illinois

Aging

Chairman,
Edward R. Roybal
California

Ranking Minority
Member,
Matthew J. Rinaldo
New Jersey

Hunger

Chairman,
Mickey Leland
Texas

Ranking Minority
Member,
Bill Emerson
Missouri

Narcotics Abuse and Control

Chairman,
Charles B. Rangel
New York

Ranking Minority
Member,
Benjamin A. Gilman
New York

Joint Committees of the United States Congress

Economic

Chairman,
Paul S. Sarbanes
Maryland

Vice Chairman,
Lee H. Hamilton
Indiana

Printing

Chairman,
Frank Annunzio
Illinois

Vice Chairman,
Wendell H. Ford
Kentucky

Library

Chairman,
Claiborne Pell
Rhode Island

Vice Chairman,
Frank Annunzio
Illinois

Taxation

Chairman,
Lloyd Bentsen
Texas

Vice Chairman,
Dan Rostenkowski
Illinois

The Central Hearing
Room of the Hart
Senate Building.

Revenue and Appropriations

The President speaks out to the Congress on Government spending during his State of the Union address.

Collecting and spending money are basic and crucial governmental powers. Under our Constitution the executive branch carries out these responsibilities, but within limits established by Congress.

The Government collects its revenues through taxes, excises, duties, customs and the sale of bonds, among other means. These monies pay for the operation of the Federal Government and the financing of Federal programs.

Article I, Section 8, of the Constitution declares that "The Congress shall have Power to lay and collect Taxes, Duties, Imposts and Excises, to pay the Debts and provide for the common Defence and general Welfare of the United States; . . ." Thus, the Congress, not the President, is empowered to impose taxes. When the Founding Fathers wrote this section of the Constitution, the memory of outrageous actions by colonial Governors was still fresh in their minds. They were determined to prevent the Executive from laying arbitrary taxes on the people. Thus, Article I, Section 7, of the Constitution states that "All Bills for raising Revenue shall originate in the House of Representatives; but the Senate may propose or concur with Amendments as on other Bills."

Under their respective rules, the responsibility for drafting tax laws lies with the Ways and Means Committee in the House and the Finance Committee in the Senate. Because their decisions directly and significantly affect the Nation's economy and the lives of virtually all Americans, these two committees are considered to be among the most powerful in Congress.

Federal agencies and departments spend money under the terms of appropriation laws and other spending laws enacted by Congress. These laws specify how much may be spent for each Government program and activity, usually during a stated period of time, often one year. As with revenue measures, the Constitution gives the appropriation powers to Congress. Article I, Section 9 states: "No Money shall be drawn from the Treasury, but in Consequence of Appropriations made by Law; and a regular Statement and Account of the Receipts and Expenditures of all public Money shall be published from time to time." By loosening the Government's purse strings or by pulling them tighter, Congress can compel executive agencies to increase or decrease their spending and thereby determine the scope of their activities.

Although the Constitution does

U.S. House of Representatives
Committee on Ways and Means
Second Session, 100th Congress

© Ed Segal—Capitol Photo Service

not explicitly empower the House to initiate appropriations bills, the House does so by custom. The Senate, as with revenue and all other measures sent to it by the House, may amend appropriations bills, increasing or decreasing amounts and inserting items of appropriation on its own initiative.

The Appropriations Committees of each House are vested with the primary responsibility for recommending spending amounts. Not surprisingly, these committees are also generally ranked among the most powerful in Congress.

In the late 1960s and early 1970s, some Members of Congress became dissatisfied with the Congressional budget process for a variety of reasons, including concern over the budgetary outcomes and the inability of Congress to respond to the President's budget proposals with comprehensive alternatives. Some felt they were left to tinker with the details, without the benefit of an overall plan.

For the most part the process was fragmented with separate decisions being made regarding tax and spending issues. In addition Congress, on the whole, did not give systematic consideration to spending priorities: what proportion of the Government's resources should go to defense, to social programs, to agriculture and so forth.

Congress responded to these criticisms in 1974 by enacting the Congressional Budget and Impoundment Control Act. This Act created a Budget Committee in each House to examine the budget, to review spending priorities and to suggest alternatives to the President's budget proposals. A nonpartisan Congressional Budget Office was established to provide Congress with budgetary information and analyses. A new procedure was set up to give Congress the opportunity to consider the budget, and a timetable was adopted to encourage the timely enactment of authorization and appropriations bills.

The timetable, along with several other provisions of the 1974 Act, was subsequently revised by the Balanced Budget and Emergency Deficit Control Act of 1985.

Since enactment of the Budget and Accounting Act of 1921, the law has required the President to take the first step in this process, preparing and submitting to Congress each January his budget recommendations for the

The Chairman and Ranking Republican Member of the Senate Appropriations Committee are John Stennis of Mississippi and Mark Hatfield of Oregon.

The President presents Congressional leaders with his 1989 Budget.

The Committee on Ways and Means, chaired by Dan Rostenkowski of Illinois, pauses for an official portrait in the Committee's hearing room.

The Federal spending process requires the close cooperation of Congressional Members from different committees. Pictured here are Representatives Leon Panetta of California, of the Budget Committee, Jamie Whitten of Mississippi, Chairman of the Appropriations Committee, and William Gray III of Pennsylvania, Chairman of the Budget Committee.

157

Revenue, appropriations and budget decisions made by these twelve Members of Congress and the six committees they lead touch the pocketbook of every American.

House Appropriations Committee

Chairman,
Jamie L. Whitten
Mississippi

Ranking Minority
Member,
Silvio O. Conte
Massachusetts

House Ways and Means Committee

Chairman,
Dan Rostenkowski
Illinois

Ranking Minority
Member,
John J. Duncan
Tennessee

House Committee on the Budget

Chairman,
William H. Gray III
Pennsylvania

Ranking Minority
Member,
Delbert L. Latta
Ohio

Senate Appropriations Committee

Chairman,
John C. Stennis
Mississippi

Ranking Minority
Member,
Mark O. Hatfield
Oregon

Senate Finance Committee

Chairman,
Lloyd Bentsen
Texas

Ranking Minority
Member,
Bob Packwood
Oregon

Senate Committee on the Budget

Chairman,
Lawton Chiles
Florida

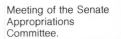

Ranking Minority
Member,
Pete V. Domenici
New Mexico

Members of the Senate
Finance Committee,
Chaired by Senator
Lloyd Bentsen of
Texas.

Meeting of the Senate
Appropriations
Committee.

entire Government. Then Congress takes over.

It sends tax proposals to the revenue committees, spending proposals to the appropriations committees and legislative proposals to the authorizing committees. The authorizing committees recommend policies and activities while the appropriations committees recommend spending amounts. Under the rules of both Houses, bills authorizing the existence of many Government agencies and activities must be acted on before appropriations for them may be considered.

Under the arrangements of the 1974 Act, each Budget Committee reviews the President's budget as well as recommendations from all other committees early in the year. The Budget Committees must report a concurrent resolution embodying their recommendations for overall budget amounts and for spending in the major functional categories. Congress is supposed to complete its consideration of this budget resolution by April 15. The purpose of the budget resolution is to set spending ceilings, a revenue floor, a deficit (or surplus) level and a public debt level. Enforcement procedures have been established to discourage efforts to spend over the ceilings or reduce revenues below the floor.

In the budget resolution the Congress may direct committees to reduce spending within laws or pending legislation within their jurisdiction. Such directions are known as reconciliation instructions; the instructions are implemented by means of one or more reconciliation bills or resolutions. Congress is scheduled to enact any reconciliation measures by June 15, although in recent years it has waited until after other budgetary decisions have been made before completing action.

Congress is supposed to complete action on appropriations bills by the beginning of each new fiscal year, October 1. This is usually accomplished by passing thirteen separate appropriations bills for various departments and combinations of departments. In the 1980s, however, Congress has had to resort increasingly to continuing resolutions to provide funding in lieu of some or all of the separate appropriations acts. For fiscal years 1987 and 1988, a single omnibus continuing resolution provided all of the appropriations for the entire government.

In the past the Budget Act requirements did not favor a particular budget policy for a fiscal year. Instead Congress determined each year whether to emphasize deficit reduction, economic stimulus or other goals in its budget policy. However, due to concern over persistent high deficits, the Congress enacted the Balanced Budget and Emergency Deficit Control Act of 1985 and, subsequently, the Balanced Budget and Emergency Deficit Control Reaffirmation Act of 1987. The revised timetable now requires the reduction of the annual deficit to zero by fiscal year 1993. If the deficit goals for each year are not met, the Act provides an automatic procedure, referred to as sequestration, to reduce spending across-the-board.

The leaders of the Senate Finance Committee are Ranking Minority Member Bob Packwood of Oregon and Chairman Lloyd Bentsen of Texas.

The Senate Budget Committee participates in setting the spending and revenue goals for the Government. Ranking Republican Member, Pete Domenici of New Mexico, and Chairman Lawton Chiles of Florida shown above.

Members of the House Appropriations Committee discuss the merits of a spending bill. Shown here are David Obey of Wisconsin, Neal Smith of Iowa, Tom Bevill of Alabama, and Bernard Dwyer of New Jersey.

The House Appropriations Committee meets to "mark up," a bill before reporting it to the floor for full consideration by the House. Pictured here are the Ranking Minority Member, Silvio O. Conte of Massachusetts, the Chairman, Jamie Whitten of Mississippi, Edward Boland of Massachusetts, and William Natcher of Kentucky.

House Budget Committee Chairman William H. Gray III of Pennsylvania.

Representative Vic Fazio of California prepares his remarks before a meeting of the Committee on Appropriations, on which he chairs the Legislative Branch Subcommittee.

Senator Robert Dole of Kansas, House Republican Leader, Bob Michel of Illinois and the Ranking Minority Member of the House Appropriations Committee, Silvio O. Conte of Massachusetts, at the deficit reduction summit in 1987.

Congress in International Affairs

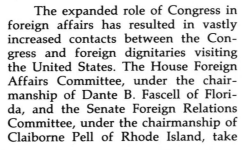

Sir Winston Churchill, Prime Minister of Great Britain, addresses a joint meeting, May 1943.

The expanded role of Congress in foreign affairs has resulted in vastly increased contacts between the Congress and foreign dignitaries visiting the United States. The House Foreign Affairs Committee, under the chairmanship of Dante B. Fascell of Florida, and the Senate Foreign Relations Committee, under the chairmanship of Claiborne Pell of Rhode Island, take the lead in welcoming these dignitaries to the Capitol and the Congress.

The Congress of the United States is a leading and influential participant in interparliamentary meetings, where discussions and policy resolutions are aimed at improving world amity, peace and the free exchange of people and ideas.

The oldest formally organized interparliamentary body is the Interparliamentary Union, established in 1889, to which all nations claiming to have parliamentary forms of government may apply for membership. The total number of nations varies from year to year but averages about 75, including several of the Eastern bloc countries. The group meets twice annually, in the spring and in the fall, with each meeting held in a different country.

The North Atlantic Treaty Organization Parliamentarians' Conference (later renamed the North Atlantic Assembly) was formed in 1955. United States participation was authorized in Public Law 689, 84th Congress, 2d Session, approved on July 11, 1956.

The North Atlantic Assembly holds two sessions each year in one of

Speaker Jim Wright has the attention of Great Britain's Prime Minister Margaret Thatcher.

Senator and Mrs. Joseph R. Biden of Delaware, during an audience with His Holiness John Paul II at the Vatican.

the NATO countries, and delegations from both Senate and House attend regularly. Committees of the Assembly meet throughout the year. Since 1981, Senator Joseph R. Biden, Jr., of Delaware has been Chairman of the Assembly's most active Committee, dealing with nuclear weapons in the Alliance.

The Canada-United States Interparliamentary Group was established by Congress under Public Law 86–42. Senator Wyche Fowler, Jr., of Georgia and Representative Sam Gejdenson of Connecticut served as Cochairmen for the Twenty-ninth Canada-United States Interparliamentary Conference in Key West, Florida, in May 1988.

The Mexico-United States Interparliamentary Group was established under Public Law 86–420. Beginning in 1961, annual conferences have been held in the United States in even-numbered years and in Mexico in odd-numbered years. Senator Christopher J. Dodd of Connecticut and Representative E (Kika) de la Garza of Texas served as Cochairmen for the Twenty-eighth Mexico-United States Interparliamentary Conference, held in New Orleans, Louisiana, in March 1988.

In addition to the above-mentioned interparliamentary groups which are specifically authorized and established by Congressional resolutions, a number of regular exchanges take place on a less formalized basis—under the general aegis of the House Committee on Foreign Affairs, the Senate Committee on Foreign Relations and the leadership of both Houses of Congress. Numerous ad hoc parliamentary delegations from many nations are received and frequently confer with Committees and their staffs, or with individual Members. In turn, Senators and Representatives are invited by foreign governments' parliamentary bodies to exchange ideas in search of greater international understanding which is essential to world peace.

Senators John Warner of Virginia and Sam Nunn of Georgia meet with Rabbi Moses Rosen of Romania. Human rights of religious minorities in Eastern bloc countries is a concern of the Congress.

Representative Dante Fascell of Florida makes a point during the Iran-Contra hearings in the summer of 1987.

U.S.-Canadian water resources matters brought Saskatchewan Premier Grant Devine to the offices of his southern neighbor, Senator Quentin Burdick of North Dakota, who is the Chairman of the Committee on Environment and Public Works.

Senator Claiborne Pell greets Israeli leader, Shimon Perez.

161

The Commission on Security and Cooperation in Europe, also known as the Helsinki Commission, is charged with monitoring human rights activities around the world. The Cochairman, Senator Dennis DeConcini of Arizona and the Chairman, Representative Steny Hoyer of Maryland, discuss trade matters with the Secretary of Commerce C. William Verity and former Commission Chairman, Senator Alphonse D'Amato of New York.

Newly elected President of the Philippines, Corazon Aquino, after a working lunch with members of the House Committee on Foreign Affairs. With Mrs. Aquino are the Chairman, Dante Fascell of Florida, Stephen Solarz of New York, Gus Yatron of Pennsylvania, and Ranking Minority Member, William Broomfield of Michigan.

A memorial service in honor of the victims of the Holocaust was held in the Capitol rotunda. Lighting the candle are Senator Claiborne Pell of Rhode Island and Representative Benjamin Gilman of New York.

El Salvador President, Jose Napoleon Duarte, speaks to Senators of his government's struggles.

Senator Claiborne Pell with former Italian Prime Minister Bettino Craxi, Italian Ambassador Rinaldo Petrignani, and Senator John H. Chafee of Rhode Island.

162

Congressional leaders meet in the Capitol with the delegation from the Soviet Union during the summit meetings on reductions of nuclear arms held in Washington in 1987. Seated around the table from left to right are Senator Robert C. Byrd of West Virginia, House Speaker Jim Wright of Texas, House Majority Leader Tom Foley of Washington, House Minority Leader Robert Michel of Illinois, House Majority Whip Tony Coelho of California, House Minority Whip Trent Lott of Mississippi, Anatoly Dobrynin, Eduard Shevardnadze, Mikhail Gorbachev, and Georgy Arbatov of the Soviet Union.

Representative Dante Fascell of Florida, Chairman of the House Foreign Affairs Committee, Representative Sid Yates of Illinois, Senator Alan Cranston of California, and Speaker of the House Jim Wright of Texas share a light moment with Soviet refusenik, Natan Sharansky, following his release from the Soviet Union and his visit to the United States in June 1986.

The annual St. Patrick's Day lunch draws sons of Erin from home and abroad.

U.S. Ambassador to Japan, former Senate Majority Leader, Mike Mansfield of Montana, poses in front of his official portrait in the Mansfield Room (Senate wing of the Capitol, second floor) with Senator Daniel K. Inouye of Hawaii and Senator Ted Stevens of Alaska.

Senators meet with West German Chancellor, Helmut Kohl. Pictured here are Caliborne Pell of Rhode Island, Robert C. Byrd of West Virginia, Sam Nunn of Georgia, Chancellor Kohl, John Warner of Virginia, and David Boren of Oklahoma.

200th Anniversary of the Signing of the Constitution

Independence Hall in Philadelphia.

On July 16, 1987, for the first time in 187 years, the United States Congress met in ceremonial session outside of Washington, D.C. Twenty-five Senators and more than 175 members of the House of Representatives traveled to Philadelphia, the seat of our Government between 1790 and 1800, for a special Congressional celebration of the Constitution's bicentennial. Included in this special delegation were the Speaker of the House, the Majority and Minority Leaders of the Senate and House, and one Member of Congress from each of the fifty States. The State delegates—12 Sena-tors and 38 Representatives—were appointed by their individual Congressional delegations. Exactly 200 years earlier, on July 16, 1787, delegates to the Federal Convention at Philadelphia broke a deadlock that had threatened to disrupt their efforts to frame a new constitution. On that day, the framers agreed to the "Great Compromise" establishing the basis of representation within the newly devised legislative branch. Under the compromise, States would be represented equally in the Senate, and in proportion to their populations in the House of Representatives.

A joint session of delegates from the 100th Congress was held in Independence Hall. In this room the U.S. Constitution was signed on September 17, 1787.

Representative Lindy Boggs of Louisiana was unanimously elected to preside over the special joint session of delegates from the House and Senate.

Senate Majority Leader Robert C. Byrd addresses the joint session.

The Speaker of the House of Representatives, Jim Wright of Texas.

House Republican Leader, Bob Michel of Illinois.

Upon the adjournment of the joint session, the House delegation moved to the House Chamber of Congress Hall for a separate proceeding. The Speaker presided over the meeting of Representatives, pictured here with their families.

Following the joint session the Senators met as a group in the Senate Chamber of Congress Hall. The presiding officer was Senator John Stennis of Mississippi, the President pro tempore of the Senate for the 100th Congress.

Senator John Melcher
of Montana, seated
next to Representative
Byron L. Dorgan of
North Dakota.

The Secretary of the
Senate, Joe Stewart,
confers with Senator
Stennis.

At the close of the
ceremonies, the retiring
of the colors.

Congress and the President

The President addresses Congress in a joint session.

The President departs the House Chamber after addressing a joint session of Congress.

The First Lady receives a warm welcome in the Executive Gallery of the House Chamber.

IN GOD WE TRUST

Courtesy of the United States Capitol Historical Society.

Presidential Inauguration

Inviation for inaugural
ceremonies sent by the
Joint Congressional
Committee on Inaugural
Ceremonies.

Since the time of Thomas Jefferson, Presidents have come to the Congress for formal inauguration. In this century a Joint Committee of Congress on Inaugural Ceremonies has been established every four years to organize the inaugural activities. The 50th Inauguration was unique because it was the first ever held in the rotunda of the Capitol. Due to sub-zero weather conditions, all outdoor activities, including the swearing-in ceremonies and the Presidential parade, were cancelled.

The 40th President of
the United States,
Ronald Wilson Reagan,
and the First Lady.

An overview of the
inaugural ceremonies in
the rotunda of the
Capitol.

Congressional Members assemble for the inaugural ceremonies.

Inaugural Committee Chairman, Charles McC. Mathias, Jr. greeting the First Lady and Mrs. Bush at the Capitol.

The President and the First Lady are escorted into the Capitol by the Speaker of the House for the 50th Inaugural Ceremonies.

The President, Vice President and Republican Leader Bob Michel.

President Reagan delivers his inaugural speech.

President Reagan takes the oath of office for his second term as President of the United States, January 21, 1985, in the rotunda of the Capitol.

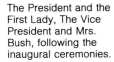

The President and the First Lady, The Vice President and Mrs. Bush, following the inaugural ceremonies.

The President and Mrs. Reagan, Vice President Bush, and the Members of The Joint

Congressional Committee on Inaugural Ceremonies 1984 - 1985.

Invitation to the
inaugural luncheon.

Congressional leaders
and guests at the
inaugural luncheon.

The President thanks
the Congress.

One of the table settings
at the inaugural
luncheon.

National Statuary Hall in
the Capitol was the site
of the Presidential
luncheon for 220 guests
following the inaugural
ceremonies.

Inaugural Chairman
Charles McC. Mathias,
Jr. presents a Steuben
glass bowl on an
engraved base to the
President.

The First Lady and Mrs.
Charles McC. Mathias,
Jr. toast the President.

House Republican
Leader Bob Michel
presents the President
with the keys to the
Capitol.

Senate photographer
presents the President
with the official
inaugural photo.

The President and the
First Lady depart for the
White House.

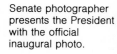

Working Relationships

The President arrives at the Capitol with the Vice President.

The President meets with Speaker Jim Wright in the Oval Office.

President Ronald Reagan addresses a joint session of Congress. Seated behind him are the Vice President and the Speaker.

The relationship between the Congress and the President is complex. Although the Constitution vests all legislative authority in the Congress, the President has important powers and responsibilities—both constitutional and customary—in the formulation and enactment of legislation. While the Constitution gives the executive authority to the President, the Congress is also empowered to check the President's actions in many ways.

The President must inform the Congress periodically on the State of the Union; he usually does so annually. The President may also transmit to Congress special messages and reports on particular subjects, and he often sends actual drafts of bills. He may exercise his veto power, threaten to do so, or appeal personally and directly to Congressional leaders and individual Members of Congress to persuade them to support his programs. His authority to adjourn Congressional sessions in case of disagreement between the two Houses has never been exercised, but he has occasionally used his power to call either or both Houses

The President and Senate Majority Leader Robert C. Byrd discuss national issues at the White House.

A distinguished club— President Ronald Reagan and former Presidents Gerald Ford, Jimmy Carter, and Richard Nixon.

The President, proud of his Irish ancestry, toasts to the health of his Congressional brethren on St. Patrick's day.

Admired for his ability to tell a good story, the President talks about Washington politics with Members of Congress.

The President is welcomed to the House side of the Capitol by Representative Silvio O. Conte of Massachusetts, and various other Congressional leaders.

The President meets in the Cabinet Room with Congressional leaders.

into special session, although rarely since the 1920s.

The President's State of the Union message to Congress receives wide public attention. Although the time, place and manner of transmitting it is discretionary with each President, he customarily delivers the message in person. Quite often it contains his views on significant matters requiring legislative attention and on the kind of legislation he wants Congress to enact. With the advent of television, this annual speech has been increasingly addressed to the people of America and of the world as well as to the Congress. It is a solemn occasion of state; modern Presidents have used it to dramatize their aims and policies and to gain Congressional support for their recommendations.

Constitutionally, the President has four courses of action when Congress submits a bill or joint resolution for his signature. He may sign it into law. He may hold it for up to ten days, whereupon, if Congress is still in session, it becomes law without his signature. If Congress adjourns during the ten-day period, the measure dies if the President has failed to sign it. This "pocket veto" is absolute and cannot be overridden by the Congress. Finally, the President may veto a measure by returning it to Congress without his signature and with a statement of the reasons for his disapproval. Congress may override the President's veto by a two-thirds vote in each House, whereupon the measure becomes law without the President's signature. If Congress does not override the veto, it will often redraft the legislation and try to work with the Administration until an agreement can be reached.

The President often meets informally with the leaders and other Members of Congress not only to discuss legislation, but also to exchange ideas and opinions on current events, problems and matters of importance to the Nation. Frequently, the President invites Members to the White House for briefings and sends his aides to Capitol Hill for the same purpose. The Congressional leadership is usually invited to the White House to be informed of major Presidential decisions and actions or important events before they are announced to the rest of the country and the world.

The relationship between the executive and legislative branches of our Government is sometimes marked with conflict, often characterized by compromise, and sometimes strained. Nevertheless, the two branches usually strive to work harmoniously for the best interests of the Nation.

Soon after the delivering the state of the Union address, the President sends to Congress his annual budget message and economic report. These are normally delivered in writing rather than in person. All Presidents send numerous other special messages to the Congress at various times during a Congressional session. Ordinarily these cover some special subject and are designed and timed to enhance support for the President's legislative agenda. Occasionally the President delivers a special message in person to emphasize the subject's vital importance. He may be warning a foreign nation of possible American reaction to its behavior, or he may be interpreting or summarizing American views for the benefit of the rest of the world.

In addition to these various messages, the President and executive agencies often send draft legislation to the Congress. Members of Congress usually introduce these items at the request of the President because neither he nor any executive official may do so.

How much effect these and other Presidential actions have in persuading Congress to accept his recommendations depends upon the circumstances. Congress is under no legal obligation to follow the President's lead, and often does not. Few major Presidential proposals survive the legislative process unchanged. Every President has learned, some with great reluctance, that negotiation and compromise are required of a President under our form of government. The sharing of power, as provided by the Constitution, makes this fact part of the American political system.

The President and Congressional leaders meet the press at the White House. Standing behind the President are House Minority Leader Bob Michel, House Majority Leader Tom Foley, Senate Republican Leader Bob Dole, Senate Majority Leader Robert C. Byrd, and House Speaker Jim Wright.

Republican Members of Congress meet with the President at the White House. Shown here are Senator Malcolm Wallop of Wyoming, the President, Senator Pete Wilson of California, Senator Dan Quayle of Indiana, House Republican Leader Bob Michel of Illinois, Representative Jack Kemp of New York, Senator Ted Stevens of Alaska, and Representative Jim Courter of New Jersey.

A short briefing with Congressional leaders before meeting with the press.

Legislative Support Agencies

Senator Claiborne Pell of Rhode Island, Chairman of the Joint Committee on the Library; Daniel J. Boorstin, Librarian of Congress Emeritus; James H. Billington, Librarian of Congress and Wendell H. Ford, of Kentucky, Chairman of the Senate Committee on Rules and Administration meet prior to a committee session.

The main reading room of the Library of Congress.

Library of Congress

The Library of Congress is believed to be the largest repository of organized knowledge in the world. It was founded in 1800 to "furnish such books as may be necessary for the use of Congress." In the gray granite structure shown on these pages, and in the neighboring John Adams and James Madison Memorial Buildings are housed 21 million books and pam-

From the miniature book collection of the Library.

James H. Billington, the Librarian of Congress.

A portion of the rare books collection.

phlets, together with more than 60 million manuscripts, maps, prints, photographs and other examples of man's graphic expression through the ages. Among the Library's greatest possessions are some of the most revered documents of American history, such as Jefferson's "rough draft" of the Declaration of Independence, one of the original copies of the Bill of Rights and the first two drafts of the Gettysburg Address in Lincoln's handwriting. From these collections can be drawn the facts that are needed to frame informed legislation.

The Library's relationship to the Congress of the United States is unique. It is an immediately accessible and indispensable tool of the Members of Congress and their committees. Its first and foremost function is to serve them. The Library furnishes facts and reports on any subject they need. Any Member or committee may borrow the book or document needed, or may have it excerpted, pinpointed or analyzed by experts on the Library staff. One department alone, the Congressional Research Service, handled more than 450,000 Congressional inquiries by phone during fiscal 1987. On a busy day, it is not unusual for more than 2,000 inquiries to be received. Many other Congressional requests are answered by the Law Library, research services, divisions and other departments.

The Library was housed in the Capitol until 1897. It suffered two disastrous fires early in its history. The entire collection of some 3,000 books was destroyed during the War of 1812, when British troops temporarily occupied Washington and burned the Capitol on August 24, 1814. Congress

promptly reconstituted the collections by purchasing the private library of Thomas Jefferson, some 6,000 volumes, on January 30, 1815. Jefferson had spent nearly 50 years assembling these books, which he had carefully organized with his own system of classification. From this new beginning the Library grew rapidly until December 24, 1851, when another fire destroyed about 35,000 volumes.

Since that time the Library's growth has been uninterrupted. The purchase in 1867 of the Peter Force collection of more than 60,000 books, pamphlets, and other items of Americana was one of a number of notable acquisitions with which Congress enriched the collections of its Library. In 1930 Congress voted $1,500,000 for the purchase of the Vollbehr Collection of 3,000 15th-century books, including the famous Gutenberg Bible,

the first book printed from movable metal type. The transfer of the library of the Smithsonian Institution to the Library of Congress in 1866, and subsequent receipts through this source, have added more than a million volumes. In 1870 Congress assigned to the Library all duties connected with copyright, insuring that it would receive a large part of the literary and artistic production of the United States. Substantial gifts from private individuals also have increased enormously the Library's resources in books and manuscripts. Finally, a network of international exchange and purchases from overseas offices have brought in material from all over the world.

This continued expansion of the collections has dictated the expansion of the Library's physical plant as well. In the spring of 1980 the Library more

During the War of 1812, the British burned the Library, which then was located in the Capitol.

James Madison Memorial Hall.

The Library of Congress Thomas Jefferson Building, with the John Adams Building at the rear.

The Great Hall in the Library of Congress.

than doubled its available space with the opening of the James Madison Memorial Building, immediately south of the main building on Independence Ave., S.E. The new building is the size of a full city block. It contains numerous reading rooms, exhibit halls and facilities for book storage, in addition to a memorial hall honoring James Madison, the chief author of the Bill of Rights and fourth President of the United States.

The Library's total inventory in 1988 amounted to 85 million items. In addition to 14 million books and pamphlets, there are more than 339,000 motion picture reels, 7 million microfilms, nearly 10 million prints and photographs and more than 36 million manuscripts relating to American history and civilization. The remainder are maps and views, music, posters and broadsides.

The Library administers the national program of library services for the blind and physically handicapped, providing since 1980 free loan of braille and talking books and magazines to millions of blind and physically handicapped persons through a nationwide network of more than 160 cooperating libraries. In addition the Library is a cultural center, where concerts and lectures are presented. It also houses the school for Capitol pages.

The Juilliard String Quartet performs frequently in the Coolidge Auditorium of the Library.

Conservator applying her craft in the conservation laboratory.

Outdoor concerts are just some of the many free cultural events of the Library.

180

The Library of Congress is an aggregate of many libraries. Its Law Library, for instance, is among the finest in the United States. Much of its usefulness stems from the fact that new legislation grows from records of the past. This was recognized early in the Library's history, when, in 1832, Congress established the law collection. Other notable collections include those of Japanese, Chinese and Russian materials, the largest outside the Orient and the Soviet Union, respectively.

James H. Billington, Russian historian and author, presides over this unique combination of facilities and services as the Librarian of Congress. Nominated by President Reagan and confirmed by the Senate, Dr. Billington was sworn into office on September 14, 1987, as the 13th Librarian of Congress in the institution's history.

The Library's first priority is service to the Congress. But its doors are open to all people. Anyone over high school age can use the Library's collections. Its exhibition halls are thronged with school children and other visitors. Its reading rooms attract scholars and students from all over the world. Its bibliographic, loan and catalog distribution services are used by the entire library world.

The Congressional Research Service

The Congressional Research Service, a department within the Library, serves as one of the research arms of the Congress. The Service was first established in 1914 for the periods during which Congress was in session. As the complexities and the burden of the problems before Congress in-creased, its staff and functions were enlarged accordingly, comprising today a staff of more than 800 persons, including selected experts in such fields as law, economics, political science, international relations, natural sciences and history. Senior specialists on the staff are frequently called upon to serve as consultants to Congressional committees.

The Director of the Service is Joseph E. Ross, former Chief of the American Law Division of CRS. Mr. Ross is a retired Navy captain and was with the U.S. Justice Department Legislative and Legal Section before joining CRS.

The Congressional Research Service, at the beginning of each Congress, prepares and presents to each Congressional committee a list of subjects and policy areas related to its concerns and also a list of programs and activities scheduled to expire during that Congress. Upon request the Service prepares legislative histories on measures to be considered in hearings; supplies committees with experts to prepare objective, nonpartisan analyses of legislative proposals that include evaluations of whether enactment of these or alternative proposals is advisable and the probable results of each; and gathers, analyzes and makes available to Members and committees other information needed in the performance of their duties. Also prepared regularly is a comprehensive digest of bills and resolutions of a public general nature introduced in either House.

CRS "hotline" handles inquiries from Congressional offices.

Some of the various publications of the Congressional Research Service.

Joseph E. Ross, Director, Congressional Research Service.

The staff of the Congressional Research Service prepares reports for Members of Congress.

Congressional Budget Office

Some of the various publications of the Congressional Budget Office.

CBO staff review computer reports on budget details.

The Congressional Budget Office (CBO) was established by the Congressional Budget Act of 1974, which also created a procedure by which the Congress considers and acts upon the annual Federal budget. This process enables the Congress to have an overview of the Federal budget and to make overall decisions regarding spending and taxing levels and the deficit or surplus these levels incur.

CBO provides Congress with basic budget data and analyses of alternative fiscal, budgetary, and programmatic policy issues. It also assists the House and Senate Budget Committees by furnishing an annual report that includes alternative spending and revenue levels and alternative allocations among major programs and functional categories, all in the light of major national needs and the effect on the balanced growth and development of the United States. CBO is headed by a director who is appointed to a four-year term by the Speaker of the House and the President Pro Tempore of the Senate, upon the recommendation of the Budget Committees.

Under the budget process the Congress establishes, by concurrent resolution, targets or ceilings and budget outlays. The Congress also establishes ceilings for the levels of revenues, the deficit, and the public debt. CBO "keeps score" for the Congress by monitoring the results of Congressional action on individual authorization, appropriation, and revenue bills against the ceilings specified in the concurrent resolution.

Since the Federal budget both affects and is affected by the national economy, the Congress must consider the Federal budget in the context of the current and projected state of the national economy. CBO therefore provides periodic forecasts and analyses of economic trends and alternative fiscal policies. CBO prepares certain budget reports on a regular basis while other studies are prepared in response to Congressional requests.

CBO staff review a committee transcript regarding Federal appropriations.

CBO is located in a Congressional Office Building along with other House Committee offices.

General Accounting Office

Comptroller General Bowsher (right) talks with Representative Vic Fazio before Congressional hearing

The General Accounting Office (GAO) was established by the Budget and Accounting Act of 1921, as an independent agency for the purpose of providing an independent audit of Government agencies. GAO is under the control and direction of the Comptroller General of the United States, who is appointed by the President with the advice and consent of the Senate for a term of 15 years.

Over the years, Congress has expanded GAO's audit authority, added new responsibilities and duties, and

GAO's Headquarters Building is the base from which its staff conducts reviews of Federal programs worldwide. Its location is convenient both to Capitol Hill and Cabinet department offices.

taken steps to increase its ability to perform independently. The basic purpose of GAO is to assist the Congress in carrying out legislative and oversight responsibilities, consistent with the role of GAO as an independent, nonpolitical agency in the Legislative Branch. GAO is also responsible for carrying out legal, accounting, auditing and claims settlement functions with respect to Federal Government programs and operations as assigned by the Congress; and to make recommendations designed to provide for more efficient and effective Government operations.

In addition to its responsibility to serve the information needs of the Congress, GAO prescribes principles and standards for accounting in Executive Branch agencies and cooperates with the agencies in developing and improving their accounting and financial management systems. GAO also settles questions concerning the legality of planned expenditure of Federal funds, questions over the award of Government contracts and requests for a Comptroller General ruling on a bid protest. GAO decisions on questions about the award of government contracts are binding on the Executive Branch but may be overturned by the Congress or the Courts.

Government Printing Office

Public Printer of the United States Ralph E. Kennickell, Jr. (left), and U.S. Senator Wendell Ford of Kentucky, Vice Chairman of the Congressional Joint Committee on Printing, hold a plate from an edition of the *Congressional Record*, one of the three daily publications produced by the GPO.

GPO (far right) is located near the Capitol and provides an array of daily services to the Congress as well as 135 other Government Customer Agencies.

The Government Printing Office (GPO) headquarters is a four-building complex located just a short distance from the U.S. Capitol. In all, 34 acres of floor space are utilized at this site. The Congressional Joint Committee on Printing oversees operations of GPO. The Public Printer, who is appointed by the President, serves as the head of the agency and is required by law to be a practical printer and versed in the art of bookbinding.

On March 4, 1861, GPO officially opened its doors for business, the same day President Lincoln was inaugurated. It has grown from a work force of 350 to some 5,000 employees nationwide. Most of these employees are based at the central office facility, making GPO the largest industrial employer in the District of Columbia.

The primary responsibility of GPO is to execute orders for printing and binding placed by Congress and departments and establishments of the Federal Government. The *Congressional Record* is one of the better known publications which is printed each day when either body of Congress is in session. Another important publication is the *Federal Register*, which contains Presidential proclamations and executive orders, as well as Federal agency regulations and notices. Other products of GPO include the *Commerce Business Daily*, United States Passports, and U.S. Postal Cards.

Although GPO is one of the world's largest general printing plants under one roof, a major portion of its work is contracted from commercial suppliers. GPO awards and administers contracts, and maintains liaison between ordering agencies and contractors.

Many of GPO's printing production systems have been modernized. It continues to shift to more sophisticated electronic technology in order to meet the specialized needs of its customers while significantly improving the efficiency of its internal operations.

GPO is the primary source of disseminating Federal information to the public, including sales through mail orders and Government bookstores consisting of approximately 17,000 different publications. It administers the depository library program through which selected Government publications are made available in libraries throughout the country as well as through the International Exchange Program.

The U.S. Government Bookstore in Kansas City is just one of 24 bookstores operated by GPO. *U.S. Government Books* and *New Books* are catalogs that list recent and popular publications for sale and can be obtained by writing to the Superintendent of Documents in Washington, DC.

Office of Technology Assessment

Chairman:
Representative Morris
K. Udall of Arizona.

Vice Chairman:
Senator Ted Stevens of
Alaska.

During the late 1960s Congress recognized the need for improving its capability to analyze the influences of science and new technology on society and Federal policy. To meet this need for non-partisan technical assistance, Congress created the Office of Technology Assessment (OTA) in 1972.

OTA is governed by a 12-member Congressional Board consisting of six Members from each House of Congress who are appointed by the President pro tempore of the Senate and the Speaker of the House. During the 100th Congress, Representative Morris K. Udall (D-Arizona) is Chairman, and Senator Ted Stevens (R-Alaska) is Vice Chairman. These posts alternate between the Senate and House with each Congress.

The Board appoints the OTA Director for a six-year term. The Director has full authority and responsibility for organizing and managing OTA's resources according to policies set by the Board. The Technology Assessment Advisory Council is comprised of 10 public members eminent in science and technology. The Council is appointed by the Board and advises OTA on assessments and other matters. The Comptroller General of the United States and the Director of the Congressional Research Service of the Library of Congress serve as ex officio members.

OTA's current studies include a broad range of complex and sophisticated technologies. This work is requested by Congressional committees and includes both classified and unclassified analyses of issues surrounding national security, technology transfer, international trade, health, energy and material resources, wastes, air and water, agriculture, and new developments such as biotechnology and programmable automation.

Assessment teams work closely with Congressional staff and support agencies to ensure that major committee concerns are addressed. OTA also draws extensively on the technical and professional resources of the private sector, including universities, research organizations, industry and public interest groups.

Throughout each project, OTA uses advisory panels of experts and representatives of major parties-at-interest as a way of ensuring that reports are nonduplicative, objective, fair and authoritative. OTA begins each year with approximately 15 new projects.

Dr. John H. Gibbons,
Director of OTA.

The OTA Congressional
Board.

In Highest Tribute

There is no more appropriate place than the rotunda of the Capitol to give honor to great servants of the people.

Flag at half mast over Capitol.

Four times in our history assassination has claimed the occupant of the White House. A forced but orderly transition took place after the tragic deaths of Abraham Lincoln, James A. Garfield, William McKinley and John F. Kennedy. All lay in state in the rotunda of the Capitol while a grieving Nation paid them tribute.

There are no known pictures of Lincoln's services in the Capitol, but there are photographs showing all of the east front columns circled with black bands and tied with large black bows to indicate that the Capitol was in mourning. After the death of Garfield on September 19, 1881, *The Evening Critic,* a Washington paper, proclaimed in black-edged columns: "God Reigns. Clouds and Darkness May Surround Us, But the Government at Washington Will Live."

No black drapery appeared on public buildings in 1901 at the time of the assassination of William McKinley. A law had been passed prohibiting such decorations because of the increasing frequency of their use to mark the deaths of minor government officials. The decorations in the rotunda planned for McKinley's lying-in-state would have been strikingly different had they been carried out. According to one newspaper report, a canopy circled with a cluster of electric lights had been built over the catafalque "so that the features of the dead President could be clearly seen" during the evening. However, a change in plans caused the viewing to close at dusk, so the electrified canopy was removed and the catafalque appeared "as it had been used by Lincoln and Garfield."

There is no law, written rule or regulation governing who may lie in state in the rotunda. Use of the rotunda is controlled, generally, by concurrent action of the Senate and House. However, the rotunda has been used without full concurrence of both Houses, especially during adjournment or recess. The wishes of the family of a great individual are also respected by Congress.

There is no more appropriate place than the rotunda of the Capitol to give honor to great servants of the people. In addition to the four Presidents who were killed while in office, there have been other Presidents and ex-Presidents accorded this same honor: Warren G. Harding in 1921, William Howard Taft in 1930, Herbert Hoover in 1964, Dwight D. Eisenhower in 1969, and Lyndon Baines Johnson in 1973. All have lain on the historic catafalque that was made for Abraham Lincoln. A total of 26 persons, including Senators, Representatives, and the Unknown Soldiers from World War I, World War II, Korea and Vietnam have lain on the catafalque in the rotunda to be given this high tribute by a grateful people.

President Jimmy Carter consoles Mrs. Hubert H. Humphrey during funeral ceremonies in the Capitol rotunda.

Military honors. The horse drawn caisson and the riderless horse with the boots turned backward are two traditional symbols in a military funeral. The flag draped casket of former President Hoover is being removed from the caisson to be carried up the Senate steps and then to the rotunda.

Those Who Have Lain in State in the Rotunda

Floral tribute. Indicative of the era when President Garfield was assassinated in 1881 were the elaborate decorations seen here around the casket in the rotunda. This particular floral arrangement is referred to as the "Gate of Heaven" and parts of it have been preserved by the Smithsonian Institution.

Henry Clay: Lay in state in the rotunda, July 1, 1852, following funeral service in old Senate Chamber. Member of U.S. Senate from Kentucky four terms (not consecutive) from 1806 to 1852; Secretary of State 1825–29; Member of House of Representatives seven terms (not consecutive) from 1811–25. During his terms in the House, he also served as Speaker, 1811–14, 1815–20, 1823–25. Died June 29, 1852, in Washington, D.C.

Abraham Lincoln: Lay in state in the rotunda, April 19–21, 1865. President of United States, March 4, 1861, until his death. Member of House of Representatives from Illinois, March 4, 1847 to March 3, 1849. Shot by assassin, April 14, 1865, in Washington, D.C., and died there April 15, 1865.

Lying in state—John Fitzgerald Kennedy.

Thaddeus Stevens: Lay in state in the rotunda, August 13–14, 1868, prior to funeral service in rotunda. Member of House of Representatives from Pennsylvania, March 4, 1849 to March 3, 1853, and again from March 4, 1859, until his death. Died August 11, 1868, in Washington, D.C.

Charles Sumner: Lay in state in the rotunda, March 13, 1874, prior to funeral service in Senate Chamber. Member of U.S. Senate from Massachusetts, April 24, 1851, until his death. Died March 11, 1874, in Washington, D.C.

Henry Wilson: Lay in state in the rotunda, November 25–26, 1875, prior to funeral service in Senate Chamber. Vice President of United States, March 4, 1873, until his death. Member of U.S. Senate from Massachusetts, January 31, 1855 to March 3, 1873, when he resigned to become Vice President. Died November 22, 1875, in Vice President's Room in Capitol, Washington, D.C.

James Abram Garfield: Lay in state in the rotunda, September 21–23, 1881, prior to funeral service in the rotunda. President of United States, March 4, 1881 until his death. Member of House of Representatives from Ohio, March 4, 1863 to November 8, 1880, when he resigned, having been elected President. Shot by assassin, July 2, 1881, in Washington, D.C., and died September 19, 1881, in Elberon, New Jersey.

John Alexander Logan: Lay in state in the rotunda, December 30–31, 1886, prior to funeral service in Senate Chamber. Member of House of Representatives from Illinois, March 4, 1859 to April 2, 1862, when he resigned to enter the Union Army, and again from March 4, 1867, until his resignation on March 3, 1871, when elected Senator. Member of U.S. Senate, March 4, 1871 to March 3, 1877. Died December 26, 1886, in Washington, D.C.

William McKinley, Jr.: Lay in state in the rotunda, September 17, 1901, following funeral in rotunda. President of United States, March 4, 1897, until his death. Member of House of Representatives from Ohio, March 4, 1877 to May 27, 1884, and again from March 4, 1885 to March 3, 1891. Shot by assassin, September 6, 1901, in Buffalo, New York, and died there September 14, 1901.

Major Pierre Charles L'Enfant (reinterment): Lay in state in the rotunda, April 28, 1909, prior to memorial service in the rotunda. Planner of city of Washington, D.C. Died June 4, 1825, and was buried on Digges farm, Prince Georges County, Maryland. Remains were brought to Capitol April 28, 1909. Remains were reinterred in Arlington National Cemetery.

Admiral George Dewey: Lay in state in the rotunda, January 20, 1917, during funeral service in the rotunda. Admiral of the Navy and hero of Manila Bay in Spanish-American War. Died January 16, 1917, in Washington, D.C.

Unknown Soldier of World War I: Lay in state in the rotunda, November 9–11, 1921. Chosen to honor and perpetuate the memory of the heroes who gave their lives in World War I. The body is that of an unknown American who served as a member of the American Expeditionary Forces in Europe and lost his life during World War I.

Warren Gamaliel Harding: Lay in state in the rotunda, August 8, 1923, following funeral service in the rotunda. President of United States, March 4, 1921, until his death. Member of U.S. Senate from Ohio, March 4, 1915 to January 13, 1921, when he resigned, having been elected President. Died August 2, 1923, in San Francisco, California.

Mrs. John F. Kennedy entering the Capitol rotunda with the late Senator Robert Kennedy of New York and Senator Edward Kennedy of Massachusetts for memorial services.

Arrival on the east front of the Capitol, with the Library of Congress and Supreme Court in the background.

189

William Howard Taft: Lay in state in the rotunda, March 11, 1930. President of United States, March 4, 1909 to March 4, 1913. Chief Justice of the United States, June 30, 1921 (commission), July 11, 1921 (oath of office) to February 3, 1930. Only man who served both as President and Chief Justice. Died March 8, 1930, in Washington, D.C.

General John Joseph Pershing: Lay in state in the rotunda, July 18–19, 1948. General of the Armies of United States. Was graduated from U.S. Military Academy at West Point in 1886 and devoted the remainder of his life to military service. Chief of Staff of the Army 1921–24; Commander of American Expeditionary Forces, World War I; distinguished service during Philippine insurrection; and took part in Spanish-American War. Died July 15, 1948, in Washington, D.C.

Robert Alphonso Taft: Lay in state in the rotunda, August 2–3, 1953, prior to memorial service in the rotunda. Member of U.S. Senate from Ohio, January 3, 1939, until his death. Died July 31, 1953, in New York City.

Unknown Soldiers of World War II and the Korean Conflict: Lay in state in the rotunda, May 28–30, 1958. Chosen to honor and perpetuate the memory of the heroes who gave their lives while serving overseas in the Armed Forces of the United States during World War II and the Korean Conflict, and whose identities are unknown.

John Fitzgerald Kennedy: Lay in state in the rotunda, November 24–25, 1963, following memorial service in the rotunda. President of United States, January 20, 1961, until his death. Member of House of Representatives from Massachusetts, January 3, 1947 to January 3, 1953. Member of U.S. Senate, January 3, 1953 to December 22, 1960, when he resigned having been elected President. Shot by assassin, November 22, 1963, in Dallas, Texas, and died there.

General Douglas MacArthur: Lay in state in the rotunda, April 8–9, 1964. Appointed General of the Army, December 18, 1944; Superintendent of U.S. Military Academy at West Point, 1919–22; appointed Chief of Staff of the Army November 21, 1930. From July 26, 1941 through April 11, 1951, he served in Pacific and Far East in various allied commands. Died April 5, 1964, in Washington, D.C.

Herbert Clark Hoover: Lay in state in the rotunda, October 23–25, 1964. President of United States, March 4, 1929 to March 3, 1933. Secretary of Commerce in cabinets of both Presidents Harding and Coolidge. Food Administrator under President Wilson, Chairman of Commission of Organization of Executive Branch of Government in 1947–49 and 1953–55. Died October 20, 1964, in New York City.

Dwight David Eisenhower: Lay in state in the rotunda, March 30–31, 1969. President of United States, January 20, 1953 to January 20, 1961. Was graduated from U.S. Military Academy at West Point in 1915; promoted to General of the Army, 1944; named president of Columbia University, 1948. Died March 28, 1969, in Washington, D.C.

Everett McKinley Dirksen: Lay in state in the rotunda, September 9–10, 1969, following memorial service in the rotunda. Member of U.S. Senate from Illinois, January 3, 1951, until his death. Member of House of Representatives, March 4, 1933 to January 3, 1949. Died September 7, 1969, in Washington, D.C.

J. Edgar Hoover: Lay in state in the rotunda, May 3–4, 1972, following memorial service in the rotunda. First Director of the Federal Bureau of Investigation, 1924 until his death. Died May 2, 1972, in Washington, D.C.

Lyndon Baines Johnson: Lay in state in the rotunda, January 24–25, 1973, following memorial service in the rotunda. President of United States, November 22, 1963 to January 20, 1969. Member of House of Representatives from Texas, April 10, 1937 to January 3, 1949. Member of U.S. Senate, January 3, 1949 to January 3, 1961, when

Lying in state—Dwight David Eisenhower.

he resigned, having been elected Vice President. Vice President, January 20, 1961 to November 22, 1963. Died January 22, 1973, at his ranch near Johnson City, Texas.

Hubert Horatio Humphrey: Lay in state in the rotunda, January 14–15, 1978. Member of U.S. Senate from Minnesota, November 3, 1970, until his death. Member U.S. Senate, January 3, 1949 to December 29, 1964, when he resigned to become Vice President, January 20, 1965 to January 20, 1969. Died at his home in Waverly, Minnesota.

Unknown Soldier of the Vietnam Era: Lay in state in the rotunda, May 25–28, 1984. Chosen to honor and perpetuate the memory of the heroes who gave their lives while serving in the Armed Forces of the United States in Southeast Asia during the Vietnam Era.

The services for the Honorable Hubert H. Humphrey were typical of the stirring simplicity of funerals in the rotunda. The precision of the military honor guard, the lines of people, and the now ever present TV camera can be considered a pattern for funerals in the Capitol rotunda.

Lying in state—Lyndon Baines Johnson.

Acknowledgement

THE CAPITOL
Ninth Edition—
100th Congress

The Successful compilation of any publication includes the efforts and talents of many individuals. While it is not possible to thank each and every person whose contributions were notable, the Joint Committee on Printing is particularly appreciative of their fine efforts.

Sam Rayburn, 1882–1961
Felix de Weldon, 1965;
bronze, 6'
Rayburn House Office
Building, main
entrance

The late Representative from Texas and long-time Speaker of the House initiated this book during the 84th Congress. The Joint Committee on Printing is proud to continue its publication.

FOR SALE BY THE SUPERINTENDENT OF DOCUMENTS,
U.S. GOVERNMENT PRINTING OFFICE, WASHINGTON, D.C. 20402

U.S. GOVERNMENT PRINTING OFFICE: 1988 O—36-700